I Am Human
30 Mistakes
To Success
Martin Johnson

big
ideas
library.

Published by The Big Ideas Library 2017

First published in the United Kingdom in 2017
by The Big Ideas Library.

The Big Ideas Library
20 Fountayne Street, York YO31
A CIP catalogue record for this book is available from the British
Library.
ISBN 978-0-9929859-8-1

Edited by Jacky Fitt
Typeset by Ned Hoste
Printed by CPI Group (UK)

The Big Ideas Library is the publishing division of
The Big Ideas Collective Ltd.

For Lucy
You have had the single greatest impact on my life. I will be forever grateful and will love you always.
Love Martin xx

For Isabel, Nyla and Zander
When you don't have the answers to some of life's questions, read this book and I'll be with you. There is a light that never goes out.
Love Dad xx

Contents

Foreword

Have you met Martin? You'd remember if you had. Martin is a force of nature.

This book is what happens when that energy is channelled into a passion to help people.

Born out of his instinctive curiosity to analyse and understand his own and others' behaviour, driven and shaped by frustration, disappointment and success, *I Am Human* is Martin's story. Mistake by mistake. It's also mine, and you'll recognise much of yourself in it too. It's our story because we're all human and, to a greater or lesser degree, we've all been there. Knowing ourselves better is the only way we're going to help ourselves and it's the key to Martin's approach.

Answering the question of why some people are able to lead contented and productive lives while others, just as able, are not, Martin begins with insight into our mental machinery and moves on to sound, practical, head-slapping staring-us-in-the-face truths and advice. Honest, intelligent and fun - sometimes a cautionary tale, sometimes a timely reminder, a kick up the bum, a light bulb moment.

Arm yourself with the 'Show Home Principle'; grab your tennis ball; drop the glass; learn about the amazing properties of bamboo and why it is that the racing driver and the heart surgeon lose the plot around Snow White.

Working with Martin on the text was intense, hilarious and hugely illuminating, and his passion for unlocking people's potential completely infectious. So, read on... Be open and honest with yourself: you already have all the tools you need to achieve what you want, Martin can show you how to use them.

It's time to get better at being human.

Jacky Fitt FRSA
Editor, *I Am Human – 30 Mistakes To Success* and award-winning author of *How to Get Inside Someone's Mind and Stay There.*

Before we begin…

You may believe in philosophical, political or religious ideologies as the route to a successful and fulfilled life. You may put your faith in science and technology to deliver our future prosperity. Yet, regardless of all our beliefs, there is one undeniable truth that connects us all…

We're all human and we rely on other humans in order to survive and thrive.

If we are to live happy, content and productive lives then first we must understand the significance and importance of our own self-fulfilment. This comes with self-awareness, knowledge and the forming of positive habits and behaviours. At its core, self-fulfilment starts with a better understanding of ourselves as unique individuals - as human beings. Only through this self-knowledge can we hope to become the best version of ourselves, enabling us to unlock our potential and, with it the ability to live a happy life. Whether we are building a business, raising a family or just trying to work out where to go next, knowledge and self-awareness are crucial.

Having interviewed, coached and worked with many thousands of people, I have identified the top 30 mistakes that we, as humans, all make and which impact our ability to truly fulfil our potential. When I say "mistakes", I mean the opportunities, strategies or learning that we have either missed, misused or misinterpreted, leading to varying degrees of toxic personal behaviour which hamper our relationships, hinder our productivity and hold us back. I speak from experience, having made just about all of them myself, and I see others struggling with these same issues every day. The good news is that by the time you have finished this book you will be in possession of all the tools you need to understand where personal self-fulfilment comes from, how we can turn our unique abilities to any goal we set and achieve the success we're looking for.

"Transcending our apparent limits is what makes us unique."
Stephen Hawking[1]

So, let's get started, but, before we can look at techniques around achieving personal success, it's very important to get to know ourselves a lot better. The first three chapters of this book are cru-cial to your personal development. From which we'll build a world of exciting possibilities. Buckle up. We're going in…

Part 1
You

"The mind is like an iceberg, it floats with one-seventh of its bulk above the water."

Sigmund Freud

Early on in my career, Freud's ideas around human brain function struck a chord with me about how human beings cope with life and work: how we externalise ourselves and behave towards each other is just a fraction of what is really going on in our minds. To find a route to greater productivity, contentment and success, we have to think of ourselves as human icebergs and dive down to look at what's happening below the waterline. It's here where we can start to work out why we think, feel, act and behave in the way that we do. I believe that without understanding more about ourselves, trying to alter our habits is nigh on impossible; ultimately, our lives will not change and the success we want will remain a frustrating pipe dream unless we can work on what's really happening at a deeper level.

First, let's get back to basics and look at what we humans are primordially programmed to do. Inherited from our primitive cave dwelling ancestors, our species has three basic functions:

1. **Survival** - To stay alive and survive

2. **Reproduction** - To find a mate and reproduce

3. **Purpose** - To have a role, a sense of belonging and contribution

Now, clearly, survival is top of the list, closely followed by reproduction and the continuation of the species, and finally, we humans tend to thrive when we have a role, a sense of belonging. We are social creatures and we need a purpose. As the first two functions have become less time-consuming and dangerous, our purpose has, and will become, ever more important to our wellbeing. So let's begin with the first of our 30 'mistakes' or, more accurately perhaps, our misconceptions and missed opportunities. It's one of the most important.

Mistake No 1
Connect with Our Sense of Purpose

Back to Freud for a second. In the 1900s he came up with an iceberg to illustrate his ideas on the model of the mind and linked human thoughts and behaviours to three levels[2]:

- **Conscious** - thoughts and perceptions above the water.

- **Preconscious** - memories, stored knowledge, fears, doubts, just below the water.

- **Unconscious -** socially unacceptable desires, selfish motives and aggression found deep down in the depths.

Fast forward to today and, inspired by Freud's ideas, the emergence of neuroscience and data gathered from my personal experience working with people in business, sport and the military, here's my version of this human iceberg. It illustrates HOW we as humans think, feel, act and behave, WHY we do so, and WHERE it all stems from.

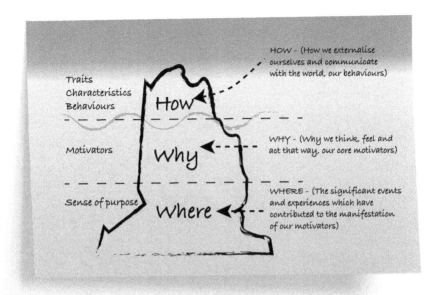

Above the waterline, in the upper section, we have our traits, characteristics and behaviours. This is HOW we externalise ourselves, how the world sees us.

Just below the waterline we have our core motivators, the reasons WHY we behave the way we do.

Deeper down, in the lower section, we have our sense of purpose. This is WHERE our core motivators are formed and is born out of the significant events of our formative years.

> **Where** on earth did that emotion come from?!
> Could that be **why** I just did that?
> OK, so here's **how** am I going to react …

I'm going to begin right down at the bottom of the iceberg with our sense of purpose, it's a fundamental part of our mindset, which drives what we do and how we go about it.

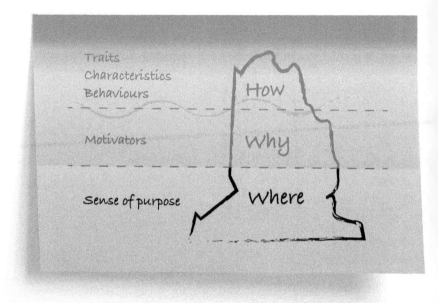

Firstly, what do I mean by sense of purpose? When we are fulfilling this we are content and productive, and this goes back to one of our core functions as a highly social species. Most performance-related discussions link back to sense of purpose, and I have found that between the ages of 1 and 16 (possibly 21 in some cases, as some of us experience impactful events up to that age), there are three critical environments which influence it:

- **Parental** – our parental influence

- **Educational** – nursery, schools, college, university or lack of it

- **Social** – culture, environment and friends

Through my work with the team at Trans2 Performance, conducting and analysing thousands of personal coaching sessions with people of all ages and from all backgrounds, sectors and expertise, it seems that these highly personal early influences and environments quite literally make us who we are. We ask questions along the lines of: "Tell me about your school years."

"Tell me about your friends." "Tell me about your dad, what did he do?" "What holidays did you go on? Where? Who did that affect and how did that make you feel?" Ultimately, we're finding out what's been going on during these formative years and why it is important or significant to you. We then reach a point where we can build a true picture of your sense of purpose.

To make this simpler to interpret and use as an effective learning tool, I have created a model that splits sense of purpose into four areas that are driven by fear and desire, or a combination of the two.

It's well known that the emotion of fear can be twice as strong a driving force as desire, which can make our anxieties far more crippling than our desires can ever be motivating. Worth a thought as we look at our sense of purpose. In the context of our four categories, have a think about where your sense of purpose may come from.

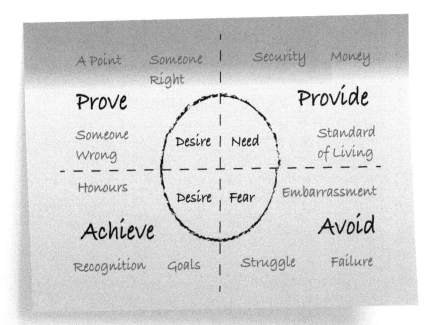

The power to PROVE - *driven by fear and desire*

One of the strongest forms of sense of purpose, when we have a point to prove, either to ourselves or someone else, and woe betide anyone who gets in the way.

"Eat my dust"

Driven by a combination of desire and fear, this sense of purpose could be based around the need to prove others wrong. This may be experiences of parents, teachers or siblings writing us off, saying we'll never amount to anything and resulting in a deep-seated sense of injustice. When we feel wronged it sticks and it stays with us. It can also work the same way if we want to prove someone right; for example, to prove our worth to parents who made big personal and financial sacrifices for us.

The drive to PROVIDE – *driven by fear and desire*

This sense of purpose is driven by the need to provide for ourselves and those that matter to us above all else.

"We will not go without"

Again, driven by both fear and desire, this is the overarching need to provide comfort and security, be that wealth, homes or material possessions but it could also include education. The drive is coming from a need to replicate or exceed a standard of living and care, or, more usually, attaining a standard that we were not fortunate enough to experience. Most importantly, ensuring that family and loved ones are provided for and sheltered.

The need to ACHIEVE – *driven by desire*

This sense of purpose is centred on gaining something tangible for our efforts. We're talking legacy. It may be in the form of academic honours like an MBA, a business recognition award, a sporting triumph or achievement.

"Remember my name"

Setting a goal and achieving it creates recognition and self-assurance, so that we can say, "I did that and nobody can take that away from me." "Those letters will be after my name forever." "The world will know that I was here." In professional sport it often becomes not about the money but about the honours. In business it's climbing the promotion ladder and status.

The desperation to AVOID – *driven by fear*

This is the most powerful sense of purpose. Driven mostly by fear, it focuses on a need to avoid embarrassment, failure or struggle at all costs. This is my primary sense of purpose and, by and large, stems from my early life experiences. For you it may include coming from a broken family, experiencing early death, drug addiction, domestic violence or adversity; having nothing, going without or being exposed to toxic or harsh environments.

"They will never suffer as I did"

This sense of purpose, at its most powerful, creates an immoveable sense of fight in a person. A real double-edged sword, it's sometimes an anger that can consume and cripple, but, if this is you and you can channel its strength, you will probably do immensely well. You will be a force to be reckoned with.

I was 11 when my father and mother separated, leaving my mother with three children to care for. We had to leave our family home and move onto a council estate. Financially we struggled. My mother did remarkably well to see us through and after leaving school with little to show for it, I joined the military at the tender age of 16. I believe that those early experiences played a big part in forming my character but it took a long time for me to gain the self-awareness needed to understand why I reacted to certain situations as I did and how that was impacting my life, as we'll go on to see in the next chapter on our core motivators.

As you build a profile of yourself you will start to understand why, on a 'good' day, there's seems to be nothing you can't do. But, on a 'bad' day, nothing goes right and the world is against you. Well, the world doesn't target individuals, so it's far more likely that you've been triggered into behaviour driven by a challenge to your sense of purpose or core motivators, and when you have that level of self-awareness you can have a re-think and get right back on track. But, before we look at our core motivators, I just want to emphasise another thing about our sense of purpose: we can have both a primary and secondary sense.

Through extensive research we have found that along with a primary sense of purpose there may also be a secondary driver. If, therefore, our primary sense of purpose is established from the ages of 1 to 21, our secondary sense of purpose is all about what's happening in the here-and-now. For example, my primary sense of purpose, which is to avoid, grew from early adversity and from that day on I have done all I can to avoid embarrassment, failure and struggle. Today, however, as I grow my business, my secondary sense of purpose is to prove. I know that every day I am proving a point to a previous employer, who, when told that I was going to set up my own business, laughed at me and said, "It's OK, you'll be back in eight weeks when it all goes wrong."

That was several years ago, yet I'm still driven to keep proving him wrong every day. I am also striving to prove a few others wrong as well! You don't forget and it's difficult to forgive someone when they undervalue and belittle you so emphatically.

My need to avoid failure and my desire to prove a point will, in all probability, not be the same as your primary and secondary sense of purpose, but you can see how the two operate together and, as life changes and we mature, our secondary sense of purpose changes over time, depending on our circumstances. We will always be blessed with our primary sense to trip us up or spur us on though.

So where does your sense of purpose come from? Taken from my research findings, here are six common examples:

1. **Lack of recognition from our father**
   Our data suggests that, as children, we crave love from our mothers and recognition from our fathers. Now, of course we need to feel love and recognition from both parents. However, what is fascinating about our one-to-one work with individuals of all ages, sexes, nationalities and from different backgrounds, was this revelation: people who grew up without receiving a good level of recognition from their father often talked about this as one of the reasons they are so driven by recognition and reward in their adult life. If they had a traditional father who had values built around being strong and independent without the need for recognition or a pat on the back, they almost always craved it as a means of self-fulfilment. This manifested in a sense of purpose to ACHIEVE.

2. **Being written off at an early age**
   We found this a common driver in people who had a sense of purpose to PROVE. If someone significant in your life has ever muttered the immortal words, "You will never amount to anything," then it is highly likely that you have a deep-seated sense of purpose and need to prove them wrong. Our studies also highlighted that this was even more prevalent if it had come from a parent or teacher.

3. **Being loved and provided for**
   We found a direct correlation between people who displayed a strong sense of purpose to PROVIDE, and a background of love, security and stability. The people who experienced this in their early life often wanted to replicate it for themselves and their family.

4. **Experiencing early adversity**
    As we have already touched on, this tends to manifest in an individual as a sense of purpose driven by the desperation to AVOID failure, embarrassment or struggle. Born out of hardships, this driver can be incredibly powerful. The stories and experiences we uncover around this include; dealing with parental separation, exposure to domestic violence, experiencing the death of a loved one, rejection and abandonment.

5. **Being inspired or encouraged by a significant someone**
    Some people have a significant person in their life. Someone who has inspired and encouraged them to ACHIEVE anything they want. This one single influence has acted as an enabler, encouraging them to set goals, achieve targets and take on anything they put their mind to.

6. **Being involved in competitive sports**
    We also found through our work around sense of purpose that there is a direct correlation between highly driven and confident individuals and the participation and exposure to competitive sport from a young age. This instills dedication to a task and the will to win and ACHIEVE.

Take a moment to think if any of the above connect with your sense of purpose?

So, if the bottom section of our iceberg is our sense of purpose, WHERE an emotion is coming from, the next level is home to our core motivators. We could describe these as our 'gut instinct', and they drive and regulate WHY we do certain things in the way that we do. As we spend our lives trying to fulfil the demands of these core motivators, it's well worth getting to know them better, and that's our next challenge.

Our Sense of Purpose

1. Our sense of purpose is born out of key events from three critical environments during our formative years. (Parental - Educational - Social)

2. We have discovered four sense-of-purpose categories. Prove - Provide - Achieve - Avoid

3. Our sense of purpose is the origin of our motivators and from which our behaviour is driven.

Mistake No 2:
Uncover Our Core Motivators

Welcome to the second level of our iceberg. Approaching the surface but still hidden from view, we find our core motivators. They have a profound impact on WHY we think, feel, act and behave in the way that we do.

At Trans2 Performance we use a personality testing tool called PRINT© licensed by the Paul Hertz Group in the US. We find this a very comprehensive and intelligent tool for identifying these core motivators, or, as PRINT© describes them, 'unconscious motivators'.

These core motivators drive our behaviour and are shaped by our early exposure and experiences (our sense of purpose). We subconsciously try to satisfy these motivators every day of our lives. If we satisfy them, then we're likely to have a good day; we're content, balanced and productive. If, however, our core motivators are challenged or compromised by someone or something, without probably even realising it we will still try to

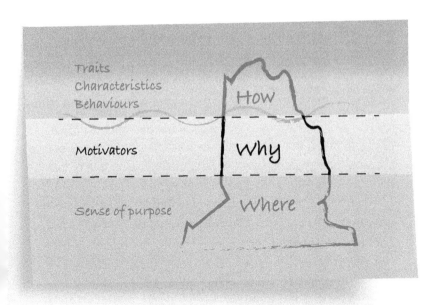

achieve them at all costs, but we feel uncomfortable, thwarted, basically pissed off and annoyed – it's a bad day and we all know what it feels like to have one of those. Nothing goes right, the world seems against us.

It's probably fair to say that 99 % of people walking the earth today don't know what their core motivators are. We may have a level of awareness of what makes us happy or unhappy, but we can't pinpoint the subtle factors that trigger our emotions and actions into either highly productive or counterproductive behaviour. That's why understanding them is very important for personal self-fulfilment and here's where, for me, PRINT© is so useful.

PRINT© was created by Dr Edwards Deming[3] (father of 'lean manufacturing' and the quality revolution in the US) and the statistician Dr Paul Hertz[4]. They wanted to understand what made people either productive or unproductive; because, quite frankly, it was no good having lean processes, or any other processes, if you had triggered, anxious and counterproductive people who weren't up to the task. It took years of research and data crunching but finally PRINT© was born as a test to drill down and discover the motivators that drive people into certain patterns of behaviour. It has been in use for the best part of a decade with government organisations, public and private businesses to great effect around the world.

The tool delivers questions that you have to answer in your core or unconscious state. The algorithms are written in such a way that you will not be able to over think or analyse your response, and your answers give your preference for one or two key motivators from a wider series of nine.

For example, my PRINT© test tells me that I need to be strong and self-reliant, and have a need to succeed. My happy place is independent, decision making, working quickly, inspiring others and coming up with ideas. I need to be fulfilling these needs every day to be content, energised and at my most productive. If, however, my core motivators are compromised or thwarted - say someone tries to curtail my independence or belittles me publicly, blocks my ideas and shuts me down – then that's where my counterproductive behaviour kicks in and it's not pretty! Guess what, I become awkward, resistant and challenging.

For a moment, let's just think back to my sense of purpose and how that has manifested in my core motivators. Through the anxious and difficult time of parental separation and the fear of going without, I grew up fast, became self-reliant. My siblings and I had to chip in and at times fend for ourselves. We learned to iron clothes, cook meals and become self-sufficient. At 16 years old I entered the military. On leaving the Royal Navy at 21 I felt more like 41 in terms of my independence and maturity. So, my sense of purpose: AVOID and PROVE, manifests in my core motivators of SUCCEED and SELF-RELIANCE – I am unconsciously driven to avoid struggle, embarrassment or failure through the experiences of my early years and therefore live in a world where I need to be self-reliant and achieve. No matter what field I work in, I must deliver the success that I feel will secure this.

Neuroscience is still working on understanding the highly complex area of brain function, but I believe that our sense of purpose and core motivators, once established, form the basis of our personalities and ability to cope with our external environments. Unlike the behaviours we display above the waterline, we have evidence that suggests our core motivators and sense of purpose are deep seated and are nigh on impossible to alter. This makes understanding them even more valuable and important as we move on to look at what the world does see and hear – the very top of the iceberg - our behaviour and actions. As I hope you can now understand, knowing what lies beneath the waterline gives us a huge advantage when it comes to approaching everyday life and dealing with the rest of the world.

Core Motivators

1. Our core motivators are thought to be formed between the ages of 1-21 through our sense-of-purpose experiences.

2. It is likely that we will have one or two core motivators regulating our behaviour.

3. Early testing shows that motivators are pretty deep-seated and relatively static, so it's worth uncovering and getting to know them better.

Mistake No 3:
Increase Our Self-Awareness

Here we are at the top of the iceberg at the third level. It's what the world sees and hears from us. It's HOW we externalise ourselves: our personality, our social style, the behaviours and traits we display.

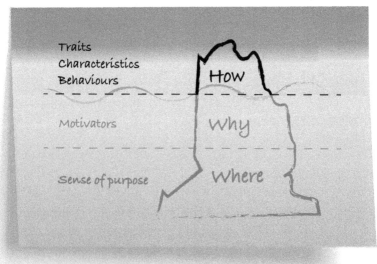

I'm sure you are quickly realising that I am fascinated by the dynamics of human behaviour. We have such a diversity of styles; introverts, extroverts, analytics, expressives, aimiables... you've got to admit we are a wonderful, complex species! But here is an interesting thing: we can't see below the waterline of other people's human icebergs so we tend to form assumptions based purely on what we see and hear - on how they act, behave and speak. Many organisations (and you may well have been involved in some of these) undertake personality testing such as DISC© or Meyers Briggs©, to get a handle on personality indicators to help support productivity and team working. These personality tests offer us some useful insight, certainly traits that we recognise about ourselves. We have our personality type confirmed and this may help us work on appropriate coping techniques, but what then?

I began Trans2 Performance because I became frustrated with the seemingly short-term benefits of traditional learning and development techniques. People would be able to make some adjustments to support their performance initially but, ultimately, reverted to type because they lacked the deeper self-knowledge that would give them the opportunity to modify how they operated from a place of powerful self-awareness. That, for me, was what was missing, the self-awareness only possible from plumbing those hidden depths of the iceberg that we have been charting to reach this point.

Now, as I've said, for me the majority of learning and development programmes and self-improvement books focus on our personality traits and our above-the-waterline behaviours. They concentrate on HOW we react to any given situation at any given time. Yet, as I've discussed in our first two mistakes, if we don't dive down deeper into our WHERE and WHY of purpose and core motivators, we have little or no chance of effective and long-lasting behavioural change and improvement. That's why so many personal development programmes are a disappointment in the long term. They may provide early gains but, if we are not addressing what's really driving our behaviour, nothing changes, nobody wins and it all feels like a waste of time.

Having conducted more than 10 years' research within business, the military and professional sport, here's what I know about our above-the-waterline behaviours:

1. **They significantly influence our perception of others and theirs of us** – how we relate to the world

2. **They can be productive and counterproductive** - in equal measure and impact.

3. **They can flex and evolve over time** – we all have the ability to change.

Importantly at this point, the words I want you to remember from these early sections are these:

The eyes are useless if the mind is blind.

What we see and hear is only our perception of others and theirs of us. If we don't understand what is driving and regulating people's behaviour then we are not seeing the full picture. To illustrate this, here's a true short story.

The CEO of a large company was very concerned about a co-worker and approached me to go through the human iceberg with his colleague. This person was highly combative, resistant to change, awkward and negative. I was the last stop before this person was to be asked to leave the company. Whether he knew it or not, I was his last hope of holding on to his job. This was a far more serious situation than I initially realised, as I would soon discover.

We began with the top of the iceberg. He felt he was a victim of his environment. He was angry and aggressive, a hostage to what he believed was his ill fortune. However, after using the PRINT© tool and drilling down further to discover his sense of purpose and core motivators, it became very clear to me why he was so combative and resistant. His early years' experience had made him highly independent and self-reliant, together with a desire to have control over his environment. He needed to feel secure, and for this reason he also liked routine. Anything that landed on him unexpectedly would trigger his defensive and challenging behaviour.

This particular person was also a director of the company, hence the impact his behaviour was having and exiting him being the last resort. After further discussion with the CEO, it also became apparent that, within the business, the director had little power to make decisions. I suggested a number of changes.

Firstly, the director should be given more control within his sphere of expertise. He should be able to make decisions and lead change. Secondly, if change was coming, the director would be brought in and given a 'heads up' a few days prior to any wider meetings. This would allow him to digest, react and challenge, as his core motivators driven by his sense of purpose kicked in, but have the time to go away and process the information in order to feel more secure. When he came back to later board meetings he would then have already thought it over, be less disruptive and bring his own ideas to the table.

The results of these changes helped to transform that company. The director has subsequently become empowered, proactive and developed a great leadership style. He is far less combative and far more supportive. The CEO was delighted. No one was fired. Productivity and profits prevailed.

However someone comes across, however we perceive them and their actions, if, as is very often the case, we don't know what is driving their behaviour, we could get our response very wrong and cause further and unnecessary distress and conflict. We have to try to understand people on a deeper level, get below the waterline, if we are truly going to be able to build long-lasting and productive relationships with them.

True self-awareness is the deeper understanding of our sense of purpose and core motivators; how they regulate our behaviour and how we come across to others as a result. Because of this, I always begin my work with individuals and teams exploring their human iceberg, and in this way avoid simply scratching the surface when seeking meaningful and lasting personal change.

Is there a pattern to our behaviour?

Now, with a deeper understanding of where our behaviour stems from (our sense of purpose) and why we act in particular ways (driven by our core motivators), I am often asked if there is a pattern in how we humans behave, or are we all completely different? Fascinatingly enough, even though we are all different and from very diverse experiences and backgrounds, I believe there is a pattern.

Throughout my studies and work, I can almost always define an individual's behaviour by one of the following:

Desire – those of us who desire certain things and outcomes and are, therefore, attracted to achievement and pleasure.

Fear – those of us who fear certain things and outcomes and are, therefore, driven by avoidance and safety.

This observation is supported by other theories, including Neuro-Linguistic Programming (NLP) which states humans are either attracted 'towards pleasure' or driven 'away from pain'. However, with my sense of purpose model and data on formative years combined with identifying core motivators, I believe we can uncover a more detailed picture of WHY some of us are attracted to or driven by desire and fear; why some of us will take risks and others won't; why some of us are a 'glass half full' and others a 'glass half empty' type of person.

It's worth pointing out at this stage that neither one of these traits is better or more productive than the other. People driven by fear are some of the most loyal, trustworthy, accurate, prepared and diligent people on the planet. Those driven by desire are some of the most committed, bold and brave people you could meet. Both have vital roles to play, both are capable of brilliance but both also have a counterproductive side of their nature. Undoubtedly, we will also all have an element of desire and fear-driven behaviour within us, but, by and large, we will resonate with one more than the other.

My answer then is, yes, there does appear to be a broad human pattern of behaviour and within that we all have productive and counterproductive sides.

Why not take a moment to put this book down and have a think about your own formative years, where your sense of purpose lies and what your core motivators may be? This, for me, is where self-awareness begins. It's our starting point to better understand, embrace and challenge ourselves, to make the most of our productive side and wrestle back more conscious control.

Increase Our Self-Awareness

1. It is through the filter of our behaviour and personality traits that others see and hear us.

2. There are many psychometric testing tools out there to help uncover our social style and behavioural preferences.

3. We find that most behaviour and traits can be characterised by the motivation to achieve success or avoid failure and pain.

Mistake No. 4:
Understand Our Social Brains

The human brain is an incredibly complex organ and we still don't have all the answers as to how it all works. However, neuroscientists and psychologists do understand the fundamentals of brain function, certainly from a social aspect. Do you think it would be a huge advantage for all of us to be more aware of what is happening in our brains as they react to what we see and hear? I do. So, Mistake Number Four is simply this: we do not take the time to learn about how our brains function, even at a basic level. This is such a missed opportunity, because I can honestly say that since I started researching and learning more about how our brains operate, especially the 'social brain', it has changed my life.

My favourite book on this subject, and one that I would highly recommend, is *The Chimp Paradox* by Steve Peters[5]. A bestseller in the vast range of personal development books available over the last five to ten years, Peters takes the complex functions of the human brain and simplifies them into how human nature relates to human behaviour – well worth a read.

Focusing purely on how we socialise: how we think, feel, act and behave; how we interact with others and how we make decisions, I'm going to run through the main points of Peters's work as it aligns with my human iceberg studies and how, with this knowledge, it may help to change your life too.

So, back to The Chimp Paradox. Peters simplifies social brain function into three particular areas, which are:

- **The Human** (The Frontal Lobe)

- **The Chimp** (The Limbic System)

- **The Computer** (The Parietal Lobe)

The Human is our frontal lobe, the prefrontal cortex, which deals largely with logic, facts and rationale. It loves data, evidence, structure and knowledge. Peters describes it as almost like our personal CEO who is going through life trying to gather data and evidence to inform us, educate us and help us come to the most accurate conclusions and decisions based on the available evidence.

The Chimp represents our limbic system. This is found deep inside our brain and will keep cropping up in this book because it's a really fascinating and influential part of our brain structure. It's incredibly active in almost all social situations, taking note of our environment, of others and providing us with our instant reactions. The limbic system hasn't got time for logic, facts and rationale. It could also be described as our 'gut instinct'. Remember our core motivators, which also, when triggered, can be thought of as a gut instinct or first response? It's working on similar lines. Have we just joined a dot there? More to come…

Our limbic system operates very much in the present. Hardwired in us since we could form a coherent thought, it is scanning the world and asking, "Friend or foe?" "Fight or flight?" "Like or dislike?" Taking decisions in seconds, it's not all about risk or warnings of impending doom: the limbic system is also responsible for our desires, exciting stuff like lust, love and attraction. It's also heavily influential in addiction and all those things that we crave. I'll look later at some brain chemicals which can supercharge the limbic system's response to our environment and external influences.

The third element of our brains highlighted by Peters and which he calls the Computer, is the parietal lobe, which sits at the top and towards the back of our heads, underneath our crown. The parietal lobe does a variety of different things, but from a social perspective it's home to our memories; it has the capacity to store our experiences as we go through life.

I'm only giving you a very brief snapshot of *The Chimp Paradox* here and, as I said, I do recommend you take the time to read the book. It really resonated with me, and we incorporate some of Peters's theories into our work at Trans2 Performance as a way to make sense of our behaviours and the 'social brain'. After all, there's no point flicking the indicators on and off: they won't help the engine run smoother when you actually need to get under the bonnet and change the oil.

OK, back to our social brain. Here's how it works. As we go through our life our Human and our Chimp are busy analysing situations and environments; one based on logic, fact and rationale, the other based on emotions and feelings. We come to our conclusions, we make our decisions, we behave in a certain way and we then store the experience in our Computer. The older we get, the more memories we store - good or bad, Peters calls these memories and experiences our 'gremlins' and 'autopilots'. But, here's the issue and the big reveal of the Peters's book. Our Chimp is FIVE TIMES QUICKER to react than our Human. Thinking back, for a moment, to our human iceberg, we acknowledge that we are all different in terms of our personalities, behaviour and characteristics. Some of us are extrovert, some introvert, etc. We have great diversity BUT what connects us all as human beings is that our limbic system fires off five times faster than the logical part of our brains.

We are ALWAYS, without exception, going to be reacting first and thinking about it later. We are all emotional animals; we can't help it.

Let's remind ourselves of our basic human functions for a

moment: survival, reproduction and purpose. Why is the limbic system, our feelings and emotions, five times quicker than the more logical part of our brain? It's down to evolution, right? But, hang on, why wouldn't evolution have made the logical part of our brain just as fast? It hasn't because of our three primary functions: survival, reproduction and purpose. Number one priority… We need lightening fast gut instinct to give us the best possible chance of escaping danger and staying alive. Think of thousands of years ago: a sabre tooth tiger walks across your path, you haven't got time to logically think to yourself, ah yes, looks like a female, about five years old, I'm probably on her territory, I wonder if she has young near by (you've been eaten by now). You have to react fast and take evasive action.

Have you ever been standing with friends in a bar or in a public place when another group or a particular individual comes in? For some reason they catch your eye and something just doesn't sit right with you. You just feel uneasy and, although your friends are talking to you, you've tuned out and your focus, even out of the corner of your eye, is on the 'threat', to the point where you have to drag your concentration back to your friends because you've missed what they've said. This heightened awareness of danger is especially prevalent in parents.

My lovely wife and I experience it with our growing family. Our sense of danger, real or perceived, has gone through the roof. It's the way our brains are programmed and I've met many people in business, working mothers and fathers, whose sense of risk and danger is heightened to the point where it's become counterproductive. If you think about it, once we find a partner and have a family, we then carry that burden of security on behalf of three or four other people at the same time. Roads are places of terrifying danger; getting on an aeroplane is harder – you've never been scared of flying but now you have your two kiddies with you, you start thinking about things that you've never thought of before. Having your partner, your children, your tribe around you, intensifies the fear and emotion around survival, while you're still trying to achieve purpose – it's exhausting! But, before we run on further, survival is still our number one instinct, which is why our limbic system, the home of our emotions and feelings, desires and fears, has to be the first thing to trigger our responses, primarily to keep us and those we protect alive.

So, back to the social brain and the limbic system which alerts us to danger, the 'fight or flight' reflex. Another example may be when you meet someone for the first time. Oddly enough, you just don't like them and you can't work out why. There's something about them, the way they talk, the volume or tone of their voice, their facial expressions and their body language. Your gut instinct kicks in and the neon sign is flashing 'Threat!' Or, more hopefully, 'Wow', this person is great, so friendly and warm, I like them, I'm going to trust them. Your first reaction takes approximately 10 seconds, which is why the old adage of never getting a second chance to make a great first impression is so true.

"You never get a second chance to make a first impression"
Will Rogers

Following our initial gut reaction, the logical part of our brain then catches up and tries to apply some rationale to back up our first limbic-generated response. Interestingly, it is rarely, if ever, to challenge that first impression: it always tries to back it up, working to gather evidence and data to support our initial reaction, pulling in memories of other experiences to reassure us that we are thinking or doing the right thing. Again, this underlines the fact that if we give a poor first impression, we then have to work twice as hard to change others' minds about us and it will take twice as long!

Now we have a little understanding of how our social brains react, let's go on to look at the chemicals which also cue changes in our behaviour towards one another.

The Chemical Soup and the Social Brain

Our thoughts and actions are also being triggered and influenced by what are known as neuro-transmitters or hormones which I'm going to describe here as brain chemicals. We must make an effort to understand these chemicals and their impact on our behaviour.

The Four Brain Chemicals

Dopamine — Desire, Drive and Motivation — — — — — —

Oxytocin — Rapport, Trust and Integrity — — —

Serotonin — Power and influence — — — — —

Cortisol — Fear, Stress amd Anxiety — —

These chemicals directly influence behaviours!

1. Dopamine

Dopamine is linked with reward and self-fulfilment and is released when we have desire, drive and motivation. If you enjoy dancing, sport or watching films for example, these activities are likely to release dopamine and you experience a sense of joy, contentment and fulfilment. Your brain will be getting a hit of dopamine when you carry out the activity and it increases your motivation to do it again. Sex releases dopamine, achieving your sales targets and (for some) completing a marathon releases dopamine. I really enjoy getting on a stage, delivering a talk and seeing people's faces and their 'light bulb' moments - that, for me, releases dopamine. It makes us want to repeat our actions time and time again. Here's another interesting thing about dopamine: addictive Class A drugs such as Heroin, Cocaine don't actually have any special ingredient as such. What they do is trigger the delivery of an overwhelming hit of dopamine, between 10-50 times more dopamine than you could ever release naturally in your greatest moment, and the only way to experience that again is to take the drug again, which is why it becomes so addictive.

In a less dramatic but also challenging way for lots of people, there is also a direct link between the sugar in our food and the triggering of dopamine in our brains. We'll feel its effects when we have one chocolate biscuit with our cup of tea. We've told ourselves that we will only have one chocolate biscuit, yet we end up eating not one but two or three more. We have crumbled because our limbic system is purring, "That tasted nice, umm, sugar release, let's do it again!" Then your logical brain responds a few minutes later in horror, "No! What did you do that for? You know it's not good for you!" And you feel rubbish because that's 500 pointless calories and you've only just had your lunch an hour ago. Dopamine is a really great thing in our lives, but we have to understand it. The goal is to try to release dopamine by doing the things that give us genuine self-fulfilment and happiness, and not eating an endless supply of chocolate biscuits or experimenting with addictive substances.

2. Oxytocin

Oxytocin has many different roles but I'm going to focus on its use in creating rapport, trust and a bond with another human being. The first major release of oxytocin in our lives comes the moment we are born, as both mother and baby receive a big hit to promote and create an instant loving bond. Your baby is the most gorgeous child on earth bar none. Now that may be true, it may not, but whatever the charms of junior, that's the oxytocin talking. It is a bonding agent. Oxytocin is also released during sex to bond two people together, and it's highly influential in any trust-based relationships.

Think about your closest circle of friends. I actually look at the three circles of love and friendship and something I will return to later in this book where I hope to make an immediate positive impact on your life. For now, think about your innermost circle: your closest allies, be it family and/or friends. You release oxytocin in their presence more than you do in anybody else's; you have something between you, an unconscious agreement that says, "We bond, you're in my circle, I trust you, I want to protect you at all costs and I know you're there for me." This is why we often jump quickly to the defence of those people. For example, if a family member is notoriously stubborn, it's fine for you to comment, but it's not fine for someone not in your inner circle to speak about them unkindly or make fun of them. Oxytocin flows when we build trust or integrity with each other. I've got your back, you've got mine.

What I observe about socially excellent people in businesses, high performers in sports teams and the best coaches and leaders is that they have an uncanny knack of influencing those around them to release oxytocin. These people have a way of gaining trust, establishing rapport, credibility and respect. They get in people's close circles very quickly and it's amazing to watch. The seemingly standoffish amongst us who tend to distance ourselves initially and radiate the message "I've got my circle… I'm not letting anybody else in" tend not to do as well socially as those who have a bigger circle or many circles. We'll come back to this later in the book.

3. Serotonin

Primarily, serotonin is linked to our sleep patterns and to digestion, our intestines and digestive system, but from a social aspect serotonin is released when we feel significant, powerful and influential within a group. It helps to maintain our confidence. Research also shows, and it's interesting to note, that low levels of serotonin in the brain are linked to depression and feelings of insignificance, worthlessness, inferiority and a lack of confidence.

What I observe in some business leaders and people in positions of power or significance is that it's all about them releasing serotonin in their own minds; it's about them feeling powerful, which is why they hit with the big stick, they micro-manage, they vilify, belittle, rant and reprimand people in public.

Great leaders, however, release serotonin in the minds of others. They empower others, they elevate others; they speak to them on a peer level; they ask them for help and ask them for their advice. One of the greatest ways to create trust, to bond and to influence others as an individual, or as a leader, is to say, "I need your help." An obvious example of this might be how Donald Trump and Barak Obama conduct themselves and the response they provoke.

It could be described as humility but it's one of the greatest things you can do to empower other people and make them feel significant and valued. If you think about all the closest people to you outside your direct family, I would be willing to bet that those people make you feel significant and valued. They show an appreciation for your great qualities. You feel great around these people because, yes, you've got oxytocin that's released so you trust them, but their response to you will also release serotonin in your brain and give you an emotional 'boost'.

We are social animals, which means we can become incredibly powerful, significant and valued human beings when we support others, far more so than if we do not. It's a lesson that some, through a misunderstanding of their sense of purpose and core motivators, never learn. It's a really important point, not to get into the trap of "It's all about me."

4. Cortisol

Say "Hello" to your greatest friend and your worst enemy! Again, cortisol has many effects on the body but, fundamentally, for our social brain, cortisol is linked to survival. When the chemical is released into our brains it's an instant response to stress, causing anxiety and fear. Our limbic systems are shouting at us "Wake up, switch on, something's wrong!" and alerting us to a potential threat.

Remember the sabre tooth tiger? At the moment you became aware of the big cat, your brain would have been flooded with cortisol, you would experience immediate heightened awareness and be poised to run, jump or climb to get to safety.

Fast forward to today. How many life-or-death situations have you been in? I'd be willing to guess not many – if any at all. I've been in one. I was on a sinking ship, which I'll get to later, but very, very few times in modern life are we exposed to an immediate life-or-death situation, so cortisol can now play an entirely and not altogether welcome role.

Cortisol is released when we feel anxious. For example, when we read a comment on Facebook that we think is aimed at us. Cortisol is released when someone comes into the office and makes a flippant remark and we think, oh no, they've got it in for me. Cortisol is released from 24-hour media reporting of terrorist acts, plane crashes, economic doom, cancer scares and natural disasters. I think the media has the balance wrong between things that are going to trigger cortisol, and things that encourage dopamine; the good news stories never make the front page if there is something scary or upsetting to report. What we are experiencing through 24-hour sensationalist news and social media is an unrelenting release of cortisol, making us anxious and stressed. Don't misunderstand me, stress does serve a purpose, it's not all bad. Acute stress is there to make us aware that things are important, are dangerous or unsafe. Chronic stress, however, is very harmful and if we go through life constantly releasing cortisol over a prolonged period, it can make us mentally and physically unwell. I don't want to class cortisol as a 'baddie', but we've got to understand its effect on our brains and have the ability to recognise and manage it accordingly.

Here are a few examples of things that have been proven to aid the reduction of cortisol release:

- **Improved diet - particularly Omega 3 fatty acids**
- **Listening to music**
- **Massage therapy**
- **Mindfulness**
- **Laughter and humour**
- **Regular exercise**

If you're feeling 'stressed out', work out how you can start to bring more of the above six things into your daily life and start to reduce the effects of cortisol. Another interesting fact about this brain chemical is the role it plays in creating and reinforcing our long-term human fears. Want to know just how crazy cortisol can make us? Here we go…

The Top 5 Global Fears

If you had to list people's worst five fears, what would you put down? Different surveys over the years taking in feedback from thousands of participants around the world, including The Washington Post, Time Inc, Researchgate.net[6], have uncovered a bizarre trend. The data showed that, although we all have different cultures, backgrounds and environments, our top fears appeared to be pretty consistent across the globe and include: death, heights, spiders, enclosed spaces, flying and financial problems. Number one, however, was the same for everyone… Public speaking.

Yes… more people would rather die than speak in public.

How bonkers is that? If we all sat down and really thought about it, I'm sure none of us would choose death over talking to a group of people, so what's going on there? Well, the reason public speaking is so feared is because of the influence of cortisol. Here's how it happens: you're about to go on stage, the limbic system fires up and says, "What the hell are you doing, this is bad!" Your heart rate increases, your blood pressure rises, your breathing speeds up because your brain is now screaming at you, telling you this is a bad idea, you're going to look stupid, you're going to forget what to say, people are going to judge you. Cortisol has now flooded your brain and you feel breathless; you have a dry mouth; you become aware of your heightened breathing and heart rate (and you think everyone else can hear it too), rational thought becomes sluggish. The cortisol impedes your ability to engage your fontal lobe and apply some logic to the situation because your limbic system doesn't want you to hang around, it wants you to run away. But the worst thing you can do is avoid your fear: you have to tackle it head-on.

The more you avoid something you fear, thinking to yourself, 'Phew. We got away with that one, the more your brain will file that feeling of relief into your memory, your parietal lobe, to be retrieved and built on at a later date. This means that when a similar situation arises, your initial anxiety actually intensifies and grows. The next time you're asked to speak in public, your brain grabs the memory, your limbic system senses 'danger', you're back reliving those unpleasant sensations and it's, "No way, I'd rather die than do that again!"

For the first three years that I delivered talks, I was terrified. It may not have appeared like it, but I came very close to giving up. After a further three years, my anxiety around public speaking became manageable; three more years of practice and honing my technique meant I started to enjoy it and now, 14 years on, I get genuine self-fulfilment when speaking to an audience with my cortisol levels well under control.

Cortisol is a really important thing to understand, recognise and manage. Public speaking is not easy but it's got to be preferable to death! We'll all have different things that strike fear into our hearts, but remember, those of us who are afraid are not inferior, we're just human - we're all just human. Do your best to face your fears head on, and through practice and repetition you will slowly start to replace the bad experiences with positive ones, replacing old neural pathways with new ones and thus conquering your fear.

Understand Brain Function

1. Understanding our social brain is incredibly important otherwise we are, in all likelihood, acting on impulse and in our unconscious, most of the time.

2. Make *The Chimp Paradox* by Steve Peters your next read.

3. Get familiar with the different brain chemicals we release and the impact they have on us and others. What can you do to start reducing your release of cortisol today?

Mistake No 5:
Open Versus Closed Loop Thinking

Closed loop thinking is an incredibly counterproductive mindset and I can honestly say that from all the people I have worked with, tested, analysed and observed, almost 100% of them get dragged into closed loop thinking at least 50% of the time, both in their personal and professional life. Make no mistake, I am just as guilty, it's human nature. So, what is closed loop thinking, why do we do it, and more importantly, why is it so damaging?

Closed loop thinking is when we pre-determine the outcome of a particular scenario, situation or event before it's even taken place; we just decide how it's going to play out. It might be a new project or product suggested at work; a new way of doing things or the revisiting of a shelved plan. Maybe your partner suggests visiting family at the weekend or it could be ideas for a night out with friends. Whatever it is, closed loop thinking brings down the shutters and bang... in an instant you have decided the likely outcome. As a result you're already tensing up as you react to this 'certainty', thinking, this is never going to work, we've tried this before or, oh boy, I can't put up with my friend's wife for an entire evening. In reality, nothing has actually happened, but in the space of a few seconds negativity has already crept in to your life and your defences are up.

Closed loop thinking is as powerful as it is destructive, because when we begin thinking in this way, our brains also unconsciously begin to gather evidence to back up or prove our flawed thought process. It's a 'reframing' of the available evidence to try to ensure we're right, to protect ourselves and our version of events, shoring up our confidence and maintaining our status by later being able to say: "I said it would be a bad idea/a rubbish night out/a waste of time and I was right."

Have a quick think about what's been happening to you over the past few days, and I am willing to bet that you will be able to come up with an example of your own closed loop thinking.

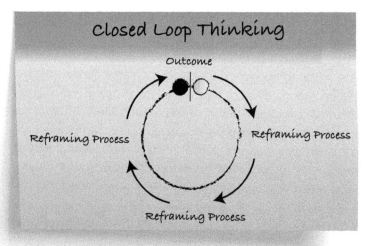

Look at the graphic above for a simplified version of how closed loop thinking gets us nowhere. Something is suggested to us. We immediately decide how it will turn out and that is our fixed point at the top of the loop. We start to move clockwise, as we encounter the actual situation, event or scenario, reframing any arguments or evidence that provide a counter argument to our initial decision, until we arrive right back where we began. We can then sit back and say "I told you so." "I knew I was right." But we've gone nowhere.

When we adopt this kind of thinking in our personal and professional life, we significantly inhibit our ability to openly engage and explore successful outcomes. We are self-sabotaging, harming ourselves and potentially having a negative impact on all of those with whom we work and live. Ultimately, we become quite a negative, dismissive person. So, what are the reasons for closed loop thinking?

1. **Learned or copied behaviour.**
   We get trapped into this mindset when we spend too much time with other closed loop thinkers: people who are always negative, know how it's all going to go wrong; can tell you all the reasons why it won't work. They write things off continually.

   There is a great Jim Rohn[7] quote which springs to mind:

   "You are the average of the five people you spend the most time with."

   If you've already started to recognise closed loop thinkers who are key influencers in your life, alarm bells should be ringing . Maybe it's time to make a change!

2. **Previous experiences.**
   As we go through life, we are gathering and storing many experiences in our parietal lobe, our memory, and if we have done something similar before that didn't work out, that pesky limbic system will, quick as a flash, come to an immediate conclusion as to why this time round it's still a bad idea or a poor choice. We all know the frustration of coming up against someone who's been there, done that, got the t-shirt and insists that they KNOW it won't work, especially if it is an area of their expertise.

3. Avoidance of accountability.

The most common reason for closed loop thinking is avoidance of accountability. If we say right from the get-go that this just isn't going to work, or it will be rubbish – "I'm not going to enjoy that holiday." – "I've done it before and it never works", then when it goes wrong we can increase our influence, look smug and utter those immortal words, "I told you so." Sadly, I see it all too often. People develop closed loop thinking because they are in survival mode. Remember our primary functions? They are stuck in first gear, self-preservation, they are reframing any arguments against their position in order not just to be right but also to totally remove themselves from any danger of accountability.

Let's just remind ourselves of my observation that 100% of human beings can get dragged into closed loop thinking up to 50% of the time. You can begin to see just how destructive this behaviour is and how it will hamper any improvement and progress in our contentment and productivity. It's fair to say that some of us are more affected by this mindset than others. Think about your core motivators. There are a couple which, if present in you, will make you more susceptible to closed loop thinking. For example, if your core motivators manifest a need within you to feel safe and secure, your brain will be constantly trying to help you avoid things going wrong and will closed loop think because it knows your primary function is to survive at all costs.

Another core motivator that leans towards closed loop thinking is perfectionism. When you need things in your life to be perfect, correct and right. When new situations come up, or as we've discussed, situations that haven't worked out before present themselves, the perfectionists' reaction may be, "If I am not fully controlling this it will not be perfect, correct and right, so I cannot commit to it. The only way I can control this is to decide what's likely to happen, make it clear from the start and then reinforce this initial view with any evidence I gather along the way". This can mean the perfectionists among us distance themselves from achieving a positive outcome or any outcome at all; they find it really hard to take a chance on something new and different.

The reality is, however, that regardless of our core motivators, we're all human and we can all fall into the trap of closed loop thinking at any point.

There's a great book called *Black Box Thinking - the surprising truth about success* by Matthew Syed[8]. In his book, Syed identifies a neurological term called Cognitive Dissonance in the same way that I am talking about closed loop thinking, and uses a very high profile example to illustrate his point.

Tony Blair and his advisors were convinced that Saddam Hussein had weapons of mass destruction and, as he believed that these posed an unacceptable threat to the civilian population and the rest of the world, we went to war with Iraq in 2003 to find and destroy them. Trouble was, no one could find them. Statements were made that they would be found, it's only a matter of time. Months go by, we turn over half the country, there are many deaths, the conflict is raging and we still haven't found a single thing. Further statements are issued in the media saying that we haven't found weapons of mass destruction yet, we're putting in more resources, more scientists, more military, give us time, it's only a matter of time. The months go by, we don't find anything.

More press releases emerge. Blair, now under scrutiny and further pressure at this point, says. "We are absolutely convinced we are on track, our intelligence tells us there are weapons of mass destruction - it's only a matter of time." Many more months go by, it's regarded as one of the worst conflicts of recent years and, ultimately, we don't find a thing. We've turned the entire country inside out at a huge human and financial cost and found nothing. Finally, after many months, Tony Blair finally concedes that no one has found weapons of mass destruction but still goes on to state that, **they must have been moved or destroyed**. He had pre-defined the outcome of the war from the start, and when it didn't turn out as predicted, he 'reframed' any contrary evidence to arrive back at the initial decision - the notion that weapons of mass destruction existed.

Closed loop thinking is an incredibly counterproductive mindset, one which is influential, stubborn, strong-willed, and above all else, a mindset which almost always means that we will reach our desired outcome, at all costs, even if its a counterproductive, narrow-minded and damaging one. Let's move on now to the far more interesting and productive process of open loop thinking and how it can change our lives.

Open Loop Thinking

I find that those people who are natural open loop thinkers, and those who regularly challenge themselves to think in this way as much as possible, are the most productive, happy and self-fulfilled people I meet. And, I say as much as possible, because none of us ever gets it right 100% of the time, we're human, right? As you can imagine, open loop is the opposite kind of mindset to closed loop thinking.

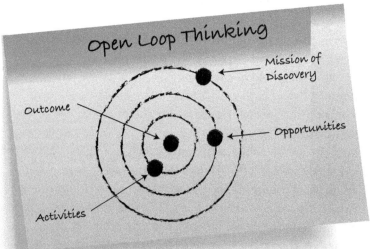

Have a look at the Open Loop thinking graphic on the previous page. Open loop thinkers work from the outside in: the outer circle is what I call the 'mission of discovery'. This is the first stage when we have been presented with a choice or a situation. At this point, open loop thinkers pause and think... hang on a second, I've got this gut feeling, my limbic system and my survival instincts are telling me this will never work, I have had a previous bad experience but BEFORE I decide on the outcome and push back, I'm going to step back and take a minute to go on the mission of discovery and sense check what my opportunities could be.

When we stop and do a quick mental mission of discovery, we give ourselves time to take into account other people's perspectives and search for any valuable knowledge and/or opportunities we could benefit from. As a result, we're now in the second circle. We're thinking about opportunities, advantages and benefits. We then move into the inner circle and start thinking about our response to the possible opportunities and the actions we must take to exploit them. Actions that, by and large, will be completely different to the reactions triggered by closed loop thinking and guess what? Using open loop thinking, time and time again, we will drive and experience completely different and far more positive outcomes. Try and remember to challenge yourself to open the loop, every day. Because...

IT will be what YOU want it to be.

We have the CHOICE to make our lives better, no matter what the situation.

A quick couple of examples: if we resist taking on a new project because it didn't work out for someone else, how can our businesses flourish? Instead of looking for reasons why something won't work, turn it on its head. Our mission of discovery may mean we actually feel the new project is a refreshing challenge because we are now in a stronger position to make it a success.

As a result, the opportunities are far more likely to open up for us.

Similarly in our personal lives. If the suggestion of spending Christmas Day with a family member doesn't appeal because a few years ago it didn't work out very well, if we are closed loop thinkers, guess what experience we'll have? We will reluctantly engage, almost determined to have a bad experience and satisfy our initial assumption. Or if we take a moment to see the benefits and opportunities of sharing or not even doing the cooking, relaxing a bit more, catching up with family, the children occupied with their cousins and the benefits offer us a much more enjoyable outcome. Because we are far more positive about the opportunities and outcome, we will have a totally different experience. We'll engage, join in and have a lot more fun. It will be what we want it to be. And that's what open loop thinkers do.

Few people are aware of this, but before I had a successful business I had a failed one. Shortly after leaving the military, my father and I started a flood protection business for homes and commercial properties. It was at a time when our region had been battered by heavy rain and flooding and it was, we thought, quite literally clean-up time – we were going to be millionaires, or so we thought. Looking back at that experience, I realise now that I was too young, too naïve, and too inexperienced to run a business well, and I made more than a couple of basic errors which resulted in the business being unprofitable. Eventually we went bust.

Fifteen years later, when I set up in business for a second time having learnt my trade in the global consulting industry, I look back at that earlier experience and, if I was a closed loop thinker, I would never have started Trans2 Performance. I would have talked myself out of it because I'd have thought, I've already tried this, I failed, I'm no good at business, it will never work out. Instead, I went on the mission of discovery to work out why my first business failed. Through this process I found that one key factor was not hiring the right people in areas where I was inexperienced, such as budgeting and cost management. Having learnt my lesson, I thought, OK, I get it, I'm comfortable with that. NOW, what are my opportunities around starting again and getting it right this time? So, second time around I opened the loop, made sure I surrounded myself with experienced, smart people and today, happily, it's a whole different story. If I'd closed the loop, I would not be writing this book for a start!

Don't make the mistake of closing the loop on your thinking. It will impact your confidence and your ability to benefit from new opportunities and live a more content, peaceful and productive life. We have to open that loop and keep it open. Without this mindset, we simply become a victim of our environment, blaming everyone and everything for the lack of our success. With open loop thinking we become the master of our destiny. Which would you rather be?

**"I am the master of my fate,
I am the captain of my soul."**

William Ernest Henley

Open vs Closed Loop Thinking

1. 100% of human beings can Closed Loop Think up to 50% of the time.

2. Closed Loop Thinking is when we pre-determine the outcome of a situation, scenario or event before it even takes place.

3. Challenge yourself to become an Open Loop Thinker. Stop yourself in your tracks, engage the logical part of your brain and go on the 'Mission of Discovery'.

Mistake No 6:

Resetting Our Expectations

When we believe that life should be fair, we create for ourselves a false interpretation of the world as it truly is. We expect positivity from everyone all of the time, and we view any kind of failure as incredibly negative and a bad reflection on us. In this world that we create, we build an assumption that we should always be happy, there can be no failure and everybody must be nice to us. You may be sat there reading this thinking, well, why the hell not? If you feel this way then you are setting yourself up for a fall and are not giving yourself the chance to develop the level of resilience we need as human beings to be happy, content and productive.

FACT: Life is not fair, nor perfect.

Thinking that life should be fair and perfect means we have unachievable and skewed expectations and it's an interesting yet rather sad evolution for us, as we've come from being the most resilient species on the planet at the top of the food chain, to jibbering wrecks if something spoils our day. There's another really good book that may be of interest about our evolution, *Sapiens – a brief history of humankind* by Yuval Noah Harari[9].

Harari explores how, over hundreds of thousands of years, Homo Sapiens has evolved from apes to become one of the most resilient species on the planet Yet today, we are arguably one of the most vulnerable. This spectacular shift is partly because of the world we live in now, but it's also down to our own skewed expectations of that world. We have created a society that is governed by such a draconian set of rules and expectations that we are conditioned and educated from childhood to view failure as bad. We have an education system that is not evolving with our needs (in fact it appears to have got stuck in the 1890s), based on a pass or fail mentality.

Marking us out from a very young age as a success or a failure significantly impacts our human resilience, because our expectation of the world is that we must have positivity and fairness all the time from everybody and we must not, we cannot, fail. We must achieve standards; we must conform to another's view of success. This kind of rigidity of thinking is crushing our personal potential and contentment and it's why I am so passionate about my work. If, on my dying day, I've made a difference to help just a few hundred people avoid this trap, I'll die a happy man!

So, if we want to be happy, succeed and achieve self-fulfilment, we must reset our expectations and build up our resilience. We will be challenged. We will get triggered into counterproductive behaviour, we will fail from time to time, but we will be prepared, because we'll understand that 'shit happens', life is not fair, nor perfect. We simply learn and move on. To put this into practice, there are two perceptions around negativity and failure we can challenge and begin to improve our resilience right now.

Two ways to improve resilience today

Learn to expect negativity from others

I'm not saying it's going to happen all the time, it doesn't, but it will happen and when it hits you and you can deal with it, you will instantly become more resilient. There are three main reasons why people may become negative towards you in your personal and professional life.

1. **Power and influence.**
   Because we live in a hierarchical society, people are negative towards us, or about us, if their status, power or influence is challenged, reinstated or elevated as a result.

2. **Core motivators.**
   As we have discovered earlier in the book, we all have different but powerful motivators that we are trying to satisfy. When these are challenged or compromised we can, if we're not careful, fall into counterproductive behaviour. We may have unconsciously triggered this in someone, hence their negative reaction - don't worry, it's not always personal.

3. **Survival instinct.**
   Again, as we've discussed earlier, one of our three primary human functions is to survive any perceived threat. When people feel in a vulnerable position, real or imagined, this translates as a threat and will fire up their limbic system and defence mechanisms. Their rational brain hasn't kicked in yet. Again, this may not be the product of an action on our part and even if it is, an initial negative reaction may change on further reflection.

When we can accept and understand that we don't live in a fair and perfect world, when faced with negative reactions, tricky situations and individuals, we can approach things in a different light and say, "OK, how am I going to get the best out of this situation, if at all?" But, whatever happens, it's not the end of the world and more often than not, it's not personal. We should expect negativity from others and understand that something else, not us, could be triggering it.

Allow ourselves room for failure

I shared with you in the last section that I had a failed business before I had a successful one and, believe me, in my current business, we have had plenty of head-scratching failures. Yet, there's a value, a lesson in everything we do; we're learning, testing and measuring all the time, enough to ensure our successes far outweigh our failures. It's important to remind ourselves that the world's most successful people experienced some kind of failure before they achieved success and acclaim. Here are three examples:

JK Rowling, the first billionaire author, sent her first manuscript based on the boy wizard Harry Potter to 12 publishers before being offered a deal. The majority of those publishers couldn't even muster the effort to send a rejection letter. One did send a Post-it note back saying: "No thank you." Sharing your creation, your concept, is a tough thing to do, and anyone without resilience or with a skewed perception of failure would have given up long before reaching number 12. We would live in a different, far less colourful world, if Rowling had.

At their first professional audition for Decca in 1962, **The Beatles**, arguably the greatest band of all time and certainly the biggest selling, were told, "Thanks but no thanks." The label preferred Brian Poole and the Tremeloes. Again, where would music be without their influence? What if they had shrugged their shoulders and said, "Well, they know best, we must be rubbish" and disbanded?

And finally, another favourite of mine…

Walt Disney, the extraordinary creator of Mickey Mouse and the Disney empire, was fired from a job with a newspaper for not being creative enough. You couldn't make it up, could you? Think of his legacy today and our other examples: they were all resilient, they took rejection, allowed themselves room for a little failure, accepted it as part of life and tried again.

The day we start to allow ourselves room for a little failure and expect negativity from others is the day we will become more resilient. What we have to overcome as individuals, entrepreneurs and leaders, is an education system of grades and conformity leading the majority of people into working lives dominated by appraisals, promotion and bonuses for the top-performing employees. The 'best' in this scenario are highly prized, the least valued will be performance-managed out and the rest, well, it's a numbing hinterland of, "You're just OK, keep going…"

I believe that when we start limiting people's beliefs by putting them into rigid ranking and scoring systems, we limit their resilience, their future abilities and productivity. It's the "succeeding is good, failure is bad," mantra but failure is not bad, because we're human, it happens. We need to redefine failure as learning and, ultimately, progress. We need to open the loop, find the opportunities from the learning and move on to better outcomes for everyone. And here's the big opportunity and what we're moving on to explore next: our IQs do not determine our success. Having left school at 16 with little to show for it and no immediate prospects or opportunities, it's a value that I live by and so can you.

Resetting Expectations

1. FACT: life is not fair, nor perfect. Understand this and acknowledge potential hardships.

2. Learn to expect negativity from others and allow yourself a little room for failure.

3. The day we expect negativity from others and allow ourselves a little room for failure, we will instantly become more resilient.

Mistake No 7:
Bringing Emotional Intelligence Into Your Conscious

I know that I am usually the most uneducated man in the room academically, but I believe I am always the most educated man in the room socially. On the whole I'd say that this statement is true of every meeting I've ever had, and probably will have throughout my career. Leaving school at 16 with little to show for it, when I sit down with people, either personally or professionally, I am aware I'm not academic. Yet, I generally feel confident that my social skills are key in supporting my success, and they're based on my ability to bring emotional intelligence into my conscious.

Emotional intelligence is a fascinating thing and it differs fundamentally from our IQ, or the intelligence quotient side of our thinking. Let's break it down.

Our IQ is a score derived from several standardised tests designed to assess human intelligence from an academic and cognitive perspective. These tests focus on the logical part of our brains: how we problem-solve, use of numbers and metrics, how we assess spatial awareness etc. As we know, some of us will naturally have an advantage by being very functional in our frontal lobe and have strong overall cognitive ability, others won't. So, IQ is a good test from an academic and cognitive perspective, but it's by no means the be all and end all when it comes to human ability.

I believe we, as a society, don't place enough value and emphasis on EQ or emotional intelligence. EQ is defined as the ability to identify, assess and control one's own emotions, the emotions of others and of groups. For me it's a key contributing factor to becoming socially excellent. This is about reading people; picking up on the conscious and unconscious signals of how another person is feeling. EQ is also about being aware of our own emotions and feelings and the ability to control them. We could argue that, as a species, EQ is fundamentally the most important aspect of brain function because we can have all the IQ and academic ability under the sun, but, if we cannot relate to and function well around others, we are not going to have the ability to form mutually beneficial relationships, be productive, happy and self-fulfilled.

Daniel Goleman[10] is an influencer of mine. An internationally renowned psychologist and science journalist for The New York Times, in 1995 Goleman wrote *Emotional Intelligence*, a ground breaking piece of work, which has sold in excess of five million copies worldwide in 40 languages. In his book Goleman describes his Emotional Intelligence Competencies Model, a simple model that splits emotional intelligence into four areas, the "four pillars of emotionally intelligent people", to help us start to understand what EQ practically means and bring it into our conscious minds.

I use Goleman's model as a template but tailor some of the content in the four pillars in line with my own findings. See overleaf:

Daniel Goleman's Emotional Intelligence
Competencies Model

Self Awareness

Emotions - Ability to tune into your own emotions and feelings, especially as you communicate.

Strengths & Limits - To recognise your own capabilities and either capitalise or build upon them.

Self Worth - Your level of self confidence has a direct correlation to the value you place on your own self worth.

1. **Self-Awareness:** how we understand ourselves in relation to others.

Emotions

When we can feel our emotional state rising or changing. We're aware that we're tired, grumpy, happy, or whatever it may be. It's very important for us to first of all recognise and be aware of what's going on within our own state of mind.

Strengths and areas to build on

I substitute the words 'weaknesses' and 'limits' here with strengths and areas to build on. A great mentor of mine always insisted that when discussing personal development we should talk about strengths and areas to build on, never strengths and weaknesses or limits. This is because an area to build on means you already can do something to a certain level, so let's build on what you already have to make it even better. The words 'weakness' and 'limit' create a mental barrier makes improvement harder. So I always like to use strengths and areas to build on. Our ability to recognise and improve our own capabilities is a big part of emotional intelligence.

Self-worth and our level of self-confidence

Self-confidence has a direct correlation to the value we place on ourselves. It cannot be externally applied, it has to come from within, we have to believe it and it manifests in the way we discuss our lives, our jobs and our potential. Emotionally intelligent people understand that and they will be accurate in their self-assessment. They're neither dramatically pessimistic nor overly optimistic, they know their true self-worth and they're confident and comfortable with themselves.

Social Awareness

Empathy - The understanding of other people's situations from their perspective, and your ability to relate to them.

Group Dynamics - Tuning in to power players and emotional undercurrents. Recognising positive and negative influencers.

Service - Recognising and meeting the needs of others.

2. **Social Awareness:** how we operate with and around others.

Empathy

People with strong emotional intelligence tend to display large amounts of empathy: the ability to genuinely understand and relate to someone else's situation from their perspective. You could say that these people are very much open loop thinkers: they rarely shut down, withdraw or live in their own worlds.

Group and power dynamics

Highly emotionally intelligent people have the ability to tune into power players and emotional undercurrents and recognise positive and negative influencers within a group. Say you're standing chatting at a party or event and there are eight people in your immediate group. If you are already tuning into who is the most dominant person, who's the most extroverted, who is maybe a little shy and struggling, then you are using your emotional intelligence. When I deliver training sessions to up to 30 people at a time, within the first 15 minutes I'm assessing group and power dynamics. I want to know who are the potential disrupters; who are the fixed mindset closed loop thinkers; who are the growth mindset open loop thinkers; who has the respect of their peers around the room; who is the socially excellent, expressive character who everybody loves being around. When I've got a handle on the group, I then tailor my approach and deliver an impactful session that allows everyone to get the most from it by engaging with each person in the most appropriate way. In organisations and leadership teams, you've got to quickly identify who are the power players, those who you need to win over to get a decision made. It's an incredibly helpful ability to learn and nurture.

Service

This is about recognising and meeting the needs of others, drawing on our empathy and what we understand of group dynamics to be able to give others what they need in order for them to feel confident. We are all at our best when we feel we are in a 'safe' space and we can go a long way to promote that through how we support others, which, as I'm sure you're realising, as with all aspects of emotional intelligence, is a key element of good leadership.

Self Management

Self Control - Ability to transfer the emotional information you have recognised, evaluate it and adapt accordingly.

Resilience - To remain optimistic and positive in an endeavour despite objection, opposition or conflict.

Open Loop Thinking - To maintain an open and growth mindset towards a particular or potential outcome.

3. **Self-management:** our ability to control ourselves.

Self-control

Using and improving this ability enables us to evaluate what we need to do in light of our empathy and group dynamics and adapt our behaviour accordingly.

Resilience

When we become aware of and increase our resilience, we have the ability to remain optimistic and positive. It's about keeping our eyes on the prize despite negativity, objection, opposition or even conflict.

Open loop thinking

In our bid to maintain our growth mindset towards a particular outcome, as we've previously discussed, open loop thinking increases our opportunities and our abilities to move forward and be more productive.

Relationship Management

Connect & Establish - Seek to understand before you demand to be understood. Connect with others and demonstrate your understanding

Influence & Inspire - Your ability to provide inspirational leadership and positively influence others.

Conflict Management - How you defuse conflicting situations and create win/win outcomes.

4. **Relationship Management:** our ability to influence and inspire others.

Connect and establish.

What I observe in emotionally intelligent people is their ability to connect to and understand others. I often use a quote from Stephen Covey's[11] *Seven Habits of Highly Effective People* when I talk about this: "Seek to understand before you demand to be understood." In other words we need to connect with others and demonstrate our understanding of them BEFORE we can hope to influence and inspire them.

Influence and inspire.

Once we have made a good connection with someone and established what their motives, ideas and requirements are, then we are far better equipped to provide leadership and positively influence them.

Conflict management

Spotting potential flash points and defusing tension and conflict is the final element. This ability allows people to appreciate and benefit from win-win outcomes and is a great building block of successful teams and businesses.

I believe we don't capitalise on the opportunity of emotional intelligence, or EQ, because we're so culturally focused on IQ and academic and cognitive abilities. We don't put as much emphasis on our so-called, 'soft skills', yet we know it has a huge impact on our ability to get on in life. For example, in February 2015 The Hay Group, a large consulting organisation based in the US, undertook a workplace survey[12] asking 300 people in the UK, 150 employers and 150 post-graduates going into employment, about the importance of emotional intelligence or 'soft skills' in the workplace versus qualifications and technical skills. From those taking part, this is what they learned.

93% of businesses believed strong soft or social skills delivered greater commercial impact.

51% of post-graduates believed that people skills got in the way of doing a job correctly.

Are you alarmed? I am. This is called a 'perception gap.' The perception of young people leaving higher education, who have for as long as they can remember been focused on passing tests and taking exams, is that qualifications are the only route to getting a good job and succeeding in the workplace. In actual fact the overwhelming majority of businesses surveyed are looking for more of a blend with an emphasis on good soft, social and people skills, because they know that's what will bring home the bacon.

Don't get me wrong, I'm not saying education is not worthwhile. Qualifications are not irrelevant, they are important, BUT, our ability to read situations and recognise our own strengths and areas to build on; to be aware of other people's emotional state and cater for their needs and adapt our responses is and will continue to be, absolutely pivotal to our personal success.

So, having highlighted Daniel Goleman's model for emotional intelligence, my question has always been: how do we bring emotional intelligence into our conscious? Through my work and research, I have found that there are three simple things we can do that will increase our emotional intelligence today.

We need to:

1. **Be present**

   We live in a world where we are preoccupied with and bombarded by social media, through our phones and devices. Add to this hectic daily routines, television and 24/7 media and, as a result, we have become less present in the company of others. It is almost impossible to be emotionally intelligent when you are not present, not focusing your full attention on someone and making eye contact. The number of times I sit in a restaurant and see couples at tables on their phones, silently looking down and not at each other is, for me, a sad confirmation that we are isolating ourselves from the skills we should be nurturing every day. Think for a moment about the people who make you feel great when you spend time with them. You'll find it's because they are present with you and you with them. To become emotionally intelligent, you have to be present.

2. **Actively listen**

   There is a difference between listening and active listening. When I'm working with people on communication skills, I always ask: "Are you truly listening to somebody or are you waiting for your turn to talk?" We all do it. I often find myself in a conversation just wanting to jump in. But we need to actively listen first. Psychologically, if we're just waiting for our turn to talk, we're not listening to a word the other person is saying.

Active listening allows us to become more emotionally intelligent. It enables us to read a situation correctly before we jump in. This can be especially true of difficult conversations. If we're having a really uncomfortable conversation with a boss or a colleague, the first things they say will trigger a reaction in us. If we do not actively listen we will have the urge to jump in, usually with a counterproductive or defensive response. We have to watch out for that quick-fire limbic system response and engage the more logical and considered element of our brain to get a full picture of what's actually going on.

3. Ask lots of questions

Too often we're eager to talk about ourselves or to promote our own agenda and we don't learn that way. We don't spot opportunities or the chance to influence another person positively. If we are present, actively listening and are asking sincere questions, with very little effort we will start to build rapport and gain trust. We will find out information that is going to allow us to tailor the conversation around subjects where both parties will gain value. Make no mistake, it has to be genuine curiosity, only then will you unearth the nuggets of useful information. The more you learn about others, the more equipped you are to build rapport, be able to be of service to that person and hopefully, in return, it will be a successful and mutually productive relationship.

People who don't take a genuine interest or have zero curiosity in others display very low levels of emotional intelligence. They don't read group situations correctly, can come across as cold or self-obsessed and, as a result, have low levels of rapport with others. They can even start saying things and acting in a way that triggers others, because they're emotionally unaware of how they're coming across.

We all like being acknowledged and understood, and if we don't bring emotional intelligence into our conscious and be present, actively listen and ask questions with genuine curiosity, we are missing out. We are not taking advantage of our opportunities to pick up on group and power dynamics and develop empathy, because how can we have empathy for someone if we don't take time to understand and get to know them?

The truly great leaders that I have had the privilege to meet and work with bring genuine empathy into everything they do. They display it in their one-to-one sessions with their team and work hard to focus on the individual and their current state of mind. Those leaders with low levels of empathy tend to stick to the numbers, objectives and goals of the business. They read the riot act but 99 times out of 100 nothing productive comes from those one-to-ones and an employee doesn't improve their performance. Without emotional intelligence we have dysfunctional workplaces and discontent in our personal lives.

Emotional Intelligence

1. Emotional Intelligence is defined as our ability to identify, assess and control our emotions, the emotions of others and of groups.

2. Emotional Intelligence consists of four areas: Self Awareness, Social Awareness, Self-Management & Relationship Management

3. To bring Emotional Intelligence into our conscious: be present - actively listen - ask more questions.

Mistake No 8:
See Things How They Are. Not Better, Nor Worse.

Let's look for a moment at unconscious versus conscious bias. One of the reasons we don't judge situations and events accurately is because we all have an unconscious bias, which is known as our implicit bias, and a conscious bias, which is our explicit bias. These manifest deep within our brains, causing us to make incredibly quick assessments of people and situations influenced by our background, cultural environment and personal experiences combined with our core motivators and, of course, our sense of purpose. There is a range of online tests that can give us guidance on where our particular bias lies.

It can be an uncomfortable process to reveal that we may have an unconscious bias towards a certain race, gender or disability, yet we all have them to a greater or lesser degree. It doesn't mean that we are sexist or racist: what the tests reveal is that at some point in our lives we experienced something that fires up in our brain when confronted with a combination of key factors – we get 'triggered' - and this can lead us to distort what we see or hear right in front of us.

On the contrary, our conscious bias is about those attitudes and beliefs that we have about a person, group or situation at a conscious level – we are fully aware of them. Most of the time these biases and how we express them come from a need to protect ourselves. They fire up because our limbic system has gone into survival mode.

Let me give you some examples of what I mean. From a business perspective, when I work with leaders on their organisational culture, more often than not I observe that the leaders always think their culture is better than it actually is, and their teams, well, they always think that it's worse. The reality is usually somewhere in the middle. The culture is not as bad as the employees make out but it's nowhere near as good as the leaders believe. This makes sense if you think about it from the leaders' perspective and their bias. The business and its culture is their baby, they created it, they see and hear what they want to and ignore what they don't. They develop both conscious and unconscious biases, they're not seeing things how they truly are, they are disengaged from their employees and they're not sorting out the issues that need addressing.

The employees, on the other hand, end up with biases from the other direction, whereby everything about the business culture is bad and the company can do no right. To be fair to everyone we need to see things how they really are, not better, nor worse, because only when we understand the reality of the situation, and what needs to be improved, can we hope to progress.

Are you a parent? We tend to have an immovable belief that our child is beautiful, well-behaved, honest and, more often than not, a misunderstood genius. We have an unconscious bias towards our children, of course we do! But as a good parent we've got to challenge our bias because we also need to guide and challenge our children. Our role is to help them grow into wonderful human beings; if they've done something wrong we need to help them correct it. If they've fallen short, we help them pick themselves up, learn from their mistakes, move on and flourish in society.

What about our friendships? Unless we have a motivator that constantly causes us to doubt ourselves, and therefore our value to others, we tend to believe that we are a better friend to our friends than they realise. We see cancelling going out with our friend on a Friday night because we're ill as the right thing to do; we won't be great company and we wouldn't want to ruin the mood – it's selfless, right? Your friend sees it as a poor excuse and that they've been let down at the last minute.

If we are to read situations correctly and, in turn, have the ability to act accordingly, we must see things how they are, not better, nor worse. Progress comes from the recognition of failings, shortcomings and unproductive behaviours and the desire to improve them. When we know the truth, warts and all, we can open the loop and improve, be that in productivity, parenting and nurturing valuable friendships that support us.

To help us see what is really going on, here's a three-step process that helps me and those I coach and work with banish the bias.

1. Ask for, welcome and embrace **feedback from others** … but here's the crucial part… the feedback can't just be from those who we want to hear from, it needs to come from those we **need** to hear from. We need to hear from the people who are unhappy or who have opposing views to us. Even from those who are not our biggest fans.

   If we want advice in our personal lives, we go to our nearest and dearest. We go to the ones we trust. We ask them how we're doing, how we look, and what do our nearest and dearest say? Usually what will make us happy, because they love us. There is value for us here because we feel supported, confident and are ready to go again. However, we need to ask the person who we know won't pull their punches and give us an honest and true reflection of what's going on. Both in our personal and professional life, feedback from others is very important if we're going to see things how they truly are.

2. Develop **self-observation.** We have to look at ourselves in as impartial a light as possible. For example, if you speak publicly, pitch or present, record yourself, watch yourself and listen to yourself. As uncomfortable as this may be at the beginning, you will spot your flaws and learn to like what you see and hear through making positive adjustments. If you're a musician or a singer, listen to yourself time and time again. If you know that you want to improve how you come across to people face-to-face, in the office or at the pub, you've got to have a level of self-observation that allows you to see and hear yourself in a light where you can start making some adjustments. When I speak I have had to make a conscious effort to correct my bad habits; to slow down and use more subtle but impactful body language. The art of seeing things how they are largely lies in self-observation.

3. Get to grips with **emotional detachment.** Maite Roel was my first female manager and someone who inspired, coached and developed me during my time working for technology consulting business Gartner. The greatest lesson Maite taught me was the power of emotional detachment.

In order to help us see things how they really are, we need to find a way to distance ourselves from ourselves if you like, to help us make sense of a dilemma. When we are personally invested in something, we often use the phrase, "I can't see the wood for the trees" and we are unable to take the right action. In this instance we need to be able to look at the situation through someone else's eyes. Here's what Maite taught me.

I was going through a really tough sales month. I was behind target and struggling. It was at the end of the sales quarter and my success, or failure, came down to one big deal, which I had been nurturing for months. The deal was making me crazy, I was acting irrationally, I was becoming a stalker but I just could not get this deal over the line. Highly stressed, I sat down with Maite a few days before the end of the quarter and related my woes, finally saying, "Maite, you need to help me, what can I do to get this deal over the line?"

She replied,: "Martin, I want you to imagine that this deal is sitting with another colleague and they are driving this opportunity. They've just told you exactly what you've told me about what's happening, what they've done so far, the situation, the dilemma… What advice would you give them?" I sat back in my chair, frustrated and I frowned at her, and said, "Well …"

Maite then repeated, "If someone else came to you in this same situation and you'd just heard it for the first time, what would you advise?" I knew what I was about to say wouldn't close the deal before the end of the quarter but it was what I truly felt, so I replied: "If I am honest Maite, I would say you've done all you can, there is clearly something wrong with this deal, it's not ready to be pushed over the line, we may have missed something. You are becoming a stalker, frankly you're going to piss them off and risk losing the deal altogether if you push any harder. My advice would be to step away and if the deal doesn't make the deadline, it doesn't make the deadline, but you need to step back and find out what's missing."

Maite looked at me and said, "There's your answer." I sort of slumped in my chair and learned in a heartbeat the power of emotional detachment. When we elevate ourselves out of a situation and look at it through the eyes of another, we will almost always arrive at the right answer.

See Things How They Are

1. You need to try to see things how they are. Not better, nor worse.

2. Be aware of unconscious and conscious bias. These can drive your thoughts and lead to skewed perceptions of reality.

3. Three tips for seeing things how they are: ask for feedback - self observation - emotional detachment.

Mistake No 9:
Stop Underselling Yourself

If we want to give ourselves the best opportunity of creating further opportunities, then we must stop underselling ourselves. Remember in the first chapter where we looked at the human iceberg? How we behave leads people to define us within moments of meeting and, therefore, they value us based on that perception.

People don't value you anywhere close to your true worth, they value you based on what they think you're worth.

Now, although we should not be deterred by what other people think, as human beings we absolutely need other people's co-operation and buy-in to succeed, so let's use this to our advantage. If people are going to value us based on what they THINK we're worth, let's make it worth their while getting to know us! Although we cannot fully control the thoughts of others, we can most definitely influence them.

My wife is a wonderful woman. She gave up her career to bring up our three children and I see her worth every single day, yet she does not. She undersells herself. She is naturally incredible. I, however, am less so, but I understand the importance of 'selling' myself and make sure that I communicate the value and credibility in everything I do, then work damn hard to back it up. Modesty can be endearing, after all who wants to talk to an arrogant, overblown narcissist? But, here's the key…. NEVER sacrifice credibility for humility.

The Power of Vulnerability[13] by Brené Brown is a great TED talk that focuses on this very subject and it's well worth a watch. I'm a great advocate of vulnerability, BUT that's not the same as allowing ourselves to be unconfident about our skills and abilities to the extent that we continually give people the wrong impression, while keeping our fingers crossed that they'll uncover the 'real' us in time. Most people simply don't have that time. Let's make it easy for them to make decisions in our favour, here's how.

We need to take control of our 'personal branding'. No one is going to blow your trumpet for you. The following statements are a few common examples of how we unintentionally undersell ourselves every day, which I'm sure you'll recognise, if not in yourself then in others.

> "I would **never be able** to stand up in front of people and give a presentation, I would **literally die. I'm not good** at speaking in public."

I understand that we may want to appear humble, display humility, even anxiety, but make this statement too many times in public and you won't be asked to speak or represent your business at any event or in any meeting. A better way to articulate this would be:

> "As **daunting** as it would be for me, I can **imagine the buzz** you get from public speaking is **amazing**."

You are still showing vulnerability and humility, but you're not shutting the door on an opportunity. Indeed you are acknowledging the power of doing something like addressing an audience and telling the other person you would be open to it, even though you would find it a challenge.

This technique highlights and uses what I term as amber, red and green language. Red language is negative and it undersells you. In our first example, words like 'never be able to', 'I'm not good' are all flashing red. Amber language is showing a little bit of vulnerability and humility and there is a place for it, mixed with green language or 'buzz words' in our example above. "As daunting as it would be " is amber language where you're getting over the fact that you would find it a challenge, which is being honest. Then using green language like 'buzz' and 'amazing' acknowledges that it would be great to do and that you're potentially up for it. You'll give a better, far more positive picture of yourself to people in this way.

Let's look at another really common example of using red versus green language. I am at a networking event and, meeting you for the first time, I ask you what you do. You reply:

> "My name is John Smith and I'm the director of a **small, niche** consulting business."

Now this may be an honest statement, humble even, but it doesn't tell me anything about the potential of the business and why I should want to ask more questions, let alone do business with you. It says to me you're small and probably too niche and narrow and therefore it's unlikely you will have any products and services for me. This kind of statement is a classic case of underselling yourself, and my first impression of you and your business is going to take a lot of effort to change on your part.

Here's what I would have said:

> "Hi, my name is John Smith and I'm the director of a **dynamic** and **fast-growing** consulting business."

It's completely honest. The company is dynamic because it's young and can be more reactive to new clients. And every time we make a sale we're growing! Using the word 'niche' gives the impression you may be a one-trick pony and you're closing doors before you've even begun. Positivity and confidence attract attention, remember no one is going to sell for you. Be honest of course, be vulnerable to a point, but always be confident about your talent and abilities, excite people about what you do and they'll always want to know more. The difference between the two statements is simply that the first is underselling the business and the person, the second is selling and enhancing the credibility of both.

In your personal life this matters just as much. Back to my wife for a moment (God she is going to kill me!) When people ask my wife what she does for a living, she replies:

"I am just a **stay-at-home** *mum."*

Now I beg to differ. She is massively underselling herself with this statement. Here's how I would describe her value:

"I have **dedicated** *the last eight years of my life to raising our children, enabling my husband to have a* **successful career***."*

We're a team and she's an immensely valuable part of our collective plan; she positively impacts mine and my children's lives, and the lives of many of our friends and families too.

We have to start selling ourselves if we want to succeed. We could look at it by thinking of ourselves as our own life-long salesman. Now, for many people 'sales' and 'marketing' are dirty words, certainly more so for us British! The reality is that all of us, every day, are in sales, so let's get over it. Let's stop underselling ourselves and have the confidence to use more amber and green words and fewer negative red words. We must kick out the pessimism and THINK about the language we use, it has a huge bearing on our ability to inspire and motivate others and encourage them to collaborate with us.

To help you make a first step, here are five universal questions that will come up time and time again throughout your life. It's a good exercise to get into the mindset of using confident, amber and green language. I've provided some example responses to illustrate the difference language makes. Then try and answer the five key questions yourself:

1. **What do you do for a living?**
   "I'm a transport manager."
   Or
   "I spend my time shipping high value goods and cargo across four continents."

2. **Tell me a bit about yourself…**
   "I live in London, married with two kids and work in a restaurant."
   Or
   "I'm a family man from London and, as a chef, I have a real passion for food and drink. One day I hope to open my own restaurant."

3. **What are you weaknesses?**
   "I'm not very confident, quite quiet and can come across as cold and unresponsive."
   Or
   "As an introvert, I'm considered in my approaches and I'm a deep thinker. This can often be mistaken for unco-operativeness."

4. **What are your strengths?**
   "Without coming across as arrogant (now you've said it, we're all thinking it) "I'd say I'm good with people and teams."
   Or

"Without a shadow of a doubt I get the greatest self-fulfilment when working with and inspiring others, that's when I come alive."

5. **What are your goals?**
"I'd like to achieve my targets at work and I'm saving up for my summer holiday next year."
Or
"Well, my dream is to take my family to Florida. If I over-achieve my sales quota by 10%, the commissions will get me there. I'm going for it!"

Each of the second responses is just as honest but much more confident and makes the person sound so much more appealing to others, and themselves. Get rid of those red words, use amber to show vulnerability, but bring in the green language to portray the best version of yourself.

The words you use, your pace, pitch and tone all have a huge bearing on your ability to positively influence others. In turn, your ability to positively influence others will have a huge bearing on your social and professional success.

You cannot influence others if you are not influenced yourself.

You cannot motivate others if you are not motivated yourself.

You certainly cannot inspire others if you are not inspired yourself.

Stop Underselling Yourself

1. People don't value us anywhere close to our true worth, they value us based on what they think we're worth.

2. Although we cannot fully control the thoughts of others, we can most definitely influence them.

3. Use green language, mixed with amber, for humility, but it's time to ditch the negative red language.

Mistake No 10:
Understand That Differences Are Only Interpretations

This is the last chapter where I'm going to be looking at YOU as an individual, and it's definitely the right one to bring this section of the book to a close. From where I sit, not appreciating another's interpretation of a situation is one of the biggest causes of unhappiness and disappointment, leading to conflict, discord and needless distress.

Just because you are right, it doesn't mean I am wrong. You just haven't seen life from my side.

We know from dissecting the human iceberg that we all have different core motivators which trigger certain behaviours, all in a bid to fulfil our sense of purpose and satisfy our values and belief systems. No one has it all figured out, we're all individuals working with very different experiences and influences. The clue here is in the word 'individual'. Most conclusions cannot be anything other than interpretations, unless it is an actual matter of fact. What I want you to take away from this short section is the unshakeable belief that we must and should appreciate another's interpretation of something and not see it as a difference. I'll put this in capitals to emphasise my point:

WE ARE ALL ALLOWED TO FORM DIFFERENT INTERPRETATIONS OF LIFE'S COMPLEXITIES.

Now, without getting too scientific or philosophical, let me give you a couple of examples of undeniable facts in our lives.

Quantities are a matter of fact. I have three children, we've created a metric system that says I, or anyone else, cannot interpret that I have more or less; it's not two, it's not four, it's three - fact. If there is a five-pound note on the table, there is a five-pound note on the table; that is a matter of fact. If I made £10,000 worth of sales this month, that's a matter of fact, it's not open for opinion or interpretation. So quantities, for me, are the first example of a fact.

Matter is another great example – the physical things that exist, that we can see and touch. Take a mobile phone, for example, it's real. Similarly a table or a chair. We can all agree it exists, we recognise it as a matter of fact.

Energy is also a matter of fact. It powers objects to move, it heats things up; it passes through things and connects things to one another. Quantities, physical things and energy are all examples in our day-to-day lives of what really can't be interpreted in any way other than what they are. However, almost everything outside these types of certainties, if you really think about it, is an interpretation. Let's have a look at some of the interpretations that most regularly create differences between us.

First up has to be politics and religion - our values and beliefs, all valid and all absolutely open to interpretation; another would be rules and territories which are created by people or groups in organisations and, as such, are an interpretation of the way things should be. Now, that doesn't mean to say we don't have to follow them. Many rules are created to help us. For example, the rules in, say, health and safety are there for our protection; the laws of our society are there to help prevent stealing, murdering or infringing civil liberties, but, ultimately, they are all just interpretations of how we, as a society, think our lives should be regulated. Success and failure is another highly contentious area.

People judge success or failure on behalf of someone else. It may be a matter of fact that a target was surpassed or not reached, the number of employees in a given department and the number of company cars in the car park, but over and above this, success and failure is all a matter of interpretation, as good, bad, right or wrong.

What's also interesting to me is that the majority of people go through life believing that most things are indeed a matter of fact and very few are open to interpretation, when in reality it's the other way around. Largely, this is down to people believing that there is only one way to achieve something. One right way (usually their way) of how it should be. This counterproductive belief system plays right into the hands of closed loop thinking It shuts down our creative and intuitive side and we need to actively flip this on its head. Remember very few things are matters of fact, and when someone does or says something that is the polar opposite of our beliefs, it's neither right nor wrong, it's just their opinion or interpretation of the situation, and guess what, it's OK.

Ten years ago, if I felt that something was not being done 'right', or as I would like it to be done, I would challenge that person or that team. Today, I would take a completely different approach. I would be far more likely to say, "That's fascinating, tell me a little bit more about why you think that way? What's your experience that led you to do it like that, and what were the results?" My motivators and experience of a situation will be different to another's and mean that we may very well approach a task from a completely different direction and, if it's not a matter of fact, everyone is allowed their opinions. It may even be a better way. That's not to say that we can't hope to persuade and influence others to our way of thinking, but we'll come to that!

Little in our world is a matter of fact: most things are just an interpretation.

It's important to nurture our ability to maintain open loop thinking: embark on the mission of discovery, come to conclusions and form ideas and opinions, but always know that it is still just our interpretation. At the same time, we must always be open to another person's point of view and try to see things from their side of life and, hopefully in return, we will receive the same consideration.

> **"We were all human until**
> **race disconnected us,**
> **religion separated us,**
> **politics divided us**
> **and wealth classified us."**
> Banksy

Differences Are Only Interpretations

1. "Just because you are right, doesn't mean I am wrong. You just haven't seen life from my side."

2. We are all allowed to form different opinions about life's complexities.

3. Very few things in this world are a 'matter of fact'. Most are indeed just our interpretation

Part 2
Your
Actions

Mistake No 11:
Simplicity Beats Complexity Every Time

A short morality tale. Back in the 1950s, the space race was in full swing with the USA and USSR vying for supremacy. Subsequently, in zero gravity, it was discovered that ink-filled pens wouldn't function and the American astronauts were having real difficulty writing up their logs and journals. NASA set its best scientists to work on the problem, and two years and millions of dollars later, a pen was created that gave uninterrupted ink flow even at zero gravity. Meanwhile, back in the USSR, the Russians... well, the Russians simply used a pencil.

OK, so this great little story isn't in fact true. It's an urban myth, but I like it because it makes an eloquent point and it's worth remembering that we, as a species, appear to be very good at solving problems that don't actually exist. Be it business processes, the use of technology or complex organisational structures, we seem to spend a lot of time and energy over-thinking and over-engineering things, basically just reinventing the wheel.

Complexity rears its ugly head in many ways in business, particularly in organisational hierarchies. In the majority of businesses I work with, I find that they have too many managers and the reason largely lies in the business trying to please people; trying to offer career progression where none exists.

We need to try to simplify everything we do. My first thought when I tackle anything in my personal and professional life is how can I simplify it? By focusing and getting clear on the following two key areas of our lives, we can make this process much more stratightforward.

1. **Our time and priorities -** What time do we have available to us and what is it important to achieve (we'll be looking more closely at how we can do this in our next chapter)? Our Associate Circle, which is everyone we know and spend time with, who is important to us and who supports us (again, I'll revisit this in more detail later in the book).

2. **Our values -** Perhaps the most important, as our values impact on everything in our lives. When we are decided about our values, our decisions become easier to make. Many successful people adopt this approach. If something doesn't align with their personal value system, they don't waste their time procrastinating or weighing up the alternatives, they move on to the next opportunity. If it aligns with their value system, it's valuable to them and they put 100% effort into making it happen. For example, driven by my core motivators, you probably won't be surprised to learn that my top three personal values are:

- **Freedom**

- **Ambition**

- **Accountability**

During my time in the military I was told what time to get up, dress and eat, see my family or even where to stand. This command and control approach has instilled in me a desire to choose for myself. Now, don't misunderstand me, my military service did great things for me at a time when I needed it: discipline, work ethic, respect, becoming socially adaptable. But, on leaving the service, my personal freedom has become very valuable to me, and woe betide anyone who tries to curtail it.

So, in order to begin simplifying your life, think about how you can better manage your time and assess your current priorities. Be aware of those who you spend time with and those who bring out the best in you, and ensure you know and put into practice a strong value system. Maybe put this book down right now and ask yourself the question: "What are my top three personal values?" Get these three elements right and you won't go far wrong. Now let's move on and look at prioritising at a deeper level.

Simplicity Beats Complexity

1. Simplicity beats complexity every time.

2. Look for ways to simplify what you do. 'Focus' for anything in life is key.

3. 2 tips for simplification: Your time and priorities - Your values. Make sure you are crystal-clear on these two, and your life will almost instantly become more straightforward.

Mistake No 12:

Prioritise and Spend Your Time Wisely

Have you ever felt like an octopus on roller skates? It's the way I describe people who don't prioritise their work. They are unfocused, unproductive and waste time. They often describe themselves as feeling constantly drained, under pressure and out of control, as their unproductive habits are making their lives at best unpredictable, at worst miserable. It's probably another way of describing a 'busy fool'. This kind of chaotic working has some pretty devastating effects too.

A crazy octopus on roller skates can't seem to concentrate for more than five minutes at a time because they have so much going on. It could be at least six, seven, or even eight things to achieve before lunch. Because of this, they seldom seem 'present' and are unable to give another person their full attention. Their cognitive ability, the way we think deeply about something, process it and then come up with a good idea or answer, is inhibited. They begin to accept lower standards just to try to get things off their 'to do list' and stem the flow of stuff coming at them from all directions. We have all probably witnessed or recognise this kind of behaviour, and the chaos only increases when the added pressure of a deadline is applied.

The Seven Habits of Highly Effective People by Steven R. Covey[14] sold in its millions on this very subject, and within it Covey offers us a really useful tool in the form of a matrix of four 'zones' in which to organise our time. You may well have come across it before, albeit in slightly different formats. Covey's matrix divides up as follows:

Urgent and important	Important but not urgent
Urgent but not important	Not important and not urgent

'**Urgent and important**' is your firefighting box containing the activities that must be done now, maybe even yesterday! You don't want to have too much in this section, but it's a fact of life.

'**Important but not urgent**' is your quality time box spent doing what's important to you, but not necessarily urgent. That's where, ideally, we want to be spending most of our time because we can give ideas, activities and projects the thinking time they deserve.

The '**urgent but not important**' box usually means it's urgent for someone else and can therefore drag us away from what we should be doing; it's a distraction. Is it something we could delegate to someone who has more time or resources?

'**Not important and not urgent**' is just that. It can wait, or should it be part of what we're doing at all? I call it the time wasting box.

By taking what we need to achieve and splitting it out in this way, it's easier to see what needs to be done when. Nothing is ever going to work perfectly, we all get distracted and things often land out of the blue, but, through using this system to manage our time and prioritise our work and lives, we can save a lot of time wasting and give ourselves clear direction about where our efforts should go.

The goal should always be to increase the quality time 'important but not urgent' part of our day and introduce some things that will support us, like watching a TED talk, going to a networking event, reading a book, taking a training course, making an ally over in HR or finance. It's a regularly heard mantra that business owners need to work more 'on' the business instead of 'in' the business, and this means putting time aside for strategic and tactical planning.

Email too is a huge distraction and needs an iron will to wrestle into submission. A very simple way to begin this is to avoid protracted email conversations. Would it be better to pick up the phone and have that conversation, or pop round and chat to that person face-to-face? When you need time to focus, turn off the email arrival sounds until you have completed what you need to do. We all know it makes sense!

Sometimes we just need to say no. I am not saying that we stop helping others out, what I am saying is that we need to be careful not to get dragged into someone else's 'urgent and important' box, and we shouldn't be afraid to say, "Hang on, I can't do this right now because..." When we do say no, however, it is really important to explain why. A flat refusal is neither helpful nor kind, and you never know when we're going to need a favour in return.

Don't be afraid to say no, as long as you are prepared to explain why.

In conjunction with the Covey Matrix, I'm also going to outline three time-management tips that I use every day to avoid becoming the dreaded octopus on roller skates.

1. **Our diaries are our statement of intent.**

   What's in your diary for the next two weeks to a month? Let's use the example of you as a sales person. When we look at your diary entries you may have three sales appointments booked in, but you also have 17 internal meetings, reviews and conference calls etc. A bunch of stuff that is not directly related to selling – or increasing your productivity. It's very important to block out time in your diary for you to focus on your primary objective, on what's going to bring home the bacon? The same principle applies to your personal life. Are you planning the activities that will give you the greatest self-fulfilment? Are you leaving enough free space in the diary for recuperation and/or spontaneous decisions? This is just as important as planned activities, as we all need down time.

2. **Use 'to do' lists.**

   Don't belittle or ignore this stalwart of organisation. For me, it's still one of the most underused life tools. I find that many people are not focusing on the activities that will drive the outcomes they need. They are accepting incoming meetings, calls and activities from others but they themselves are not initiating this activity. In effect they are a hostage to fortune, instead of being in control of their life. Are you focusing on and driving the activities that are going to deliver the outcomes you desire, or are you being side-tracked and joining somebody else's journey? Get YOUR 'to do' list sorted every morning then apply it to the Covey Matrix. A mentor of mine once spelt it out for me, "Do what you need to do today, today, then get your arse over to the quality time box!"

3. **Say "no".** The ability to say "Sorry, but no" will enable us to execute the first and second points here effectively. We have to sometimes, when needed, be able to say "no", and, to do this effectively we must be prepared to explain why. If you just say "no", you become negative and will be perceived as unreasonable and that will be personally damaging, but I have never met a boss or a leader – a good leader – who doesn't appreciate someone guarding their time appropriately in order to do a better job.

In order to become more productive, we must always be conscious of how we are spending our time. We must take charge of our lives and make sure we are doing the things that will bring us self-fulfilment and allow us to reach our goals. Are you walking your own path, or are you following someone else's?

Prioritise and Spend Time Wisely

1. Read *The 7 Habits of Highly Effective People* and check out the Covey Matrix for time management.

2. Use 'To Do' lists. it is the most underrated and underused time management system in business and in life. But…do what you need to do today, today!

3. Don't be afraid to say 'No' to people, as long as you are prepared to explain why.

Mistake No 13:
Make Better Decisions

Our decisions chart our direction through life; the actions we take, our behaviour towards others, hundreds and hundreds of decisions every day making small differences or major impacts, they are central to our success. Let's lift the lid now on how we, as humans, make decisions and, perhaps more importantly, how we can give ourselves the best chance of making the right ones for us.

Over the years I have collated a body of research in decision-making. From working with corporate buyers to better understand how they make key investment decisions, to how we, as individuals, set our personal goals and make key life decisions. Through that research, I have discovered a pattern.

There are four key factors of decision-making, whether you are buying a house or a type of cheese, deciding to start a business, write a book or run a marathon. Once we know the four factors, we need to bring them into our conscious if we are to make better decisions for ourselves and influence those of others.

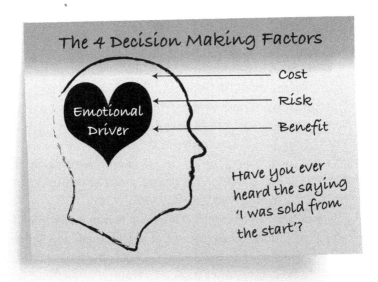

The 4 Decision Making Factors

Emotional Driver

Cost
Risk
Benefit

Have you ever heard the saying 'I was sold from the start'?

1. **COST** Time and/or money. How much time do I have to invest in this? How much money do I have to invest? Can I afford the time and/or money to take this course of action?

2. **RISK** What are the risks to me of making this decision, or, indeed, not making it? As we explored earlier in this book, our limbic system is hardwired to react within moments of a perceived risk to us with a release of the brain chemical cortisol. This makes it difficult at times to make big decisions, we become hesitant because of a perceived risk, we get ourselves tied up in knots and our thinking gets clouded.

3. **BENEFIT** What are the known personal or financial rewards that I'll reap from making this decision, what value will I get from my choice?

   These three drivers, cost, risk and benefit, all feature in any decision that we make. However, it's actually the fourth driver that is the most powerful ingredient in the mix, eclipsing all others, and it's one that is present in every single decision we make.

4. **EMOTIONAL DRIVER** The emotional driver overrides the other three every time and is by far the biggest influence on the decisions we make. So, when making decisions we must be aware of this and tap into it if we want to make the right ones for us.

Here's a personal example of the emotional driver in action. I call this the 'Show Home Principle', and believe me I've been a victim of this twice in my life… you think I'd learn, right?

My wife and I have been living in a great house, quite content, it's a perfectly good house and we're happy. Then, one Saturday afternoon, my wife says, "Oh, we've got some time, let's go down the road and see what those new houses are like. I'm told they do the interiors out really well. Let's just go and have a look. Maybe get some ideas for our home." So we go and, of course, the show home is amazing because they kit it out with the best kitchens, bathrooms and furniture – beautiful things that make my wife and I immediately visualise our lives in that house: all the family round for Christmas, summers in the expansive garden, colder nights snuggled around the log burner, lots of space in the walk-in wardrobe… The emotional driver starts to kick in, my wife wants it, bloody hell even I want it now! Forty-five minutes later I'm sitting down with a sales representative doing a deal on a brand new house that two hours earlier we didn't know we needed. We only went out for a walk!

A show home is a superb selling tool, bringing not just the building but also the lifestyle alive in the mind of the buyer. This is a principle I teach to sales teams, it's all about bringing your product or service alive in the mind of the buyer (but that's a different book…).

So how did the 'Show Home Principle' blindside me twice? Yes, I thought about the cost of a higher mortgage, the risk of taking this on with a young family and fledgling business, I appreciated the benefit of more space and being closer to great schools, BUT when my emotional driver kicked in and flooded my brain with dopamine, making me feel excited and alive, the other three factors took a back seat. I wanted that house for myself, for my wife and my children. I was sold on it from the moment I walked in: all the salesman had to do was sit me down and justify the cost, risk and run over the benefits one more time – the deal was done.

When our emotional driver kicks in, things happen. When we're not emotionally connected, or we haven't got an emotional driver that says, "I want this", we will procrastinate. So, what are great decisions or better decisions? How can we make better decisions knowing what we do about our four key drivers?

Bad decisions can happen when we have an overriding emotional driver - we act on impulse and we don't pay any or enough attention to the cost, risk or benefits. Bad decisions can ALSO happen when we make a decision based purely on cost, risk and benefit and we have no emotional connection to it. I find that the best decisions are taken when we feel content and comfortable because the decision process is led by our emotional driver and we have also taken the time to assess and satisfy ourselves about the costs, risks and benefits. We've got to understand what's happening to us when we get excited about a deal, an offer or an idea. We've got to remember how we're made and think, yep, here come all my emotions, it's completely natural and I'm excited. Good. Now I'm going to check out the other factors that will make this decision good for me or not. And don't forget that advertisers know this!

I use three decision-making formulas to illustrate my point:

1. **Benefits** minus **risk** plus cost with NO emotional driver = this could be a good decision, but it may not be – I'm unsure, I'm procrastinating, in fact I'm not that excited by it.

2. **Emotional driver** ONLY = lets go for it, I'm excited, it will be fine. (a bit later on…) oh dear, can we afford this, not sure it was sensible. Regret!

3. **Emotional driver** plus **benefits** minus **risk** plus **cost**
   = we almost always make a decision because we'll
   manage the costs somehow - I'll work some extra hours,
   I'll do a deal, I'll take a dividend, I'll do something …
   but it feels like a great decision because we've gone
   through the process, we're excited by it and we've
   reassured ourselves that it's the right thing to do.

Always be aware, when you make a decision that's all about
emotional connection and is, therefore, solely emotionally driven,
it's a very short-term buzz. You may regret it, and that's the last
thing you want.

The most content people I know make decisions based on
emotional drivers because that's what they want for themselves
or their families, BUT they also ensure they support their emotional reaction with the assurance of the right level of costs, risks
and benefits. If you want to make great decisions, make sure you
satisfy all four decision-making drivers. If you want to influence
other people to make decisions, first and foremost fire up their
emotional driver and back it up with the benefits off-setting their
potential risk and investment.

Make Better Decisions

1. In order to make better decisions, we need to
   understand the main factors in play.

2. The four decision-making factors are: Cost - Risk -
   Benefit - Emotional Driver.

3. The emotional driver is without doubt the most
   influential factor in decision making. Remember 'The
   Show Home Principle'? Great decisions are made
   when led by our emotional driver, but reinforced with
   due diligence on the cost, risk and benefit.

Mistake No 14:
Leveraging Resources and Becoming Resourceful

Resources and resourcefulness are two entirely different things and productive people, people who seem to overcome challenges and achieve what they want, combine their use of resources and their own resourcefulness very, very well.

Resources are the things that we have available to us to be able to do our jobs, to fulfil our requirements, achieve whatever it is in life – office or studio facilities, technology, staff, equipment, transport etc. And, quite often, we don't have all the resources that we would like, certainly if you're starting out as a young entrepreneur or start-up business. Even if you're doing the bucket list stuff in your life but you don't have the money, knowledge or confidence, such as wanting to run a marathon but you don't have any running shoes or the know-how to train properly, sometimes we want to do things but we don't have all the resources.

Now, there are a lot of people out there who blame a lack of resources for their lack of achievement. In the workplace, people often talk negatively about their careers: they dread going to work on a Monday morning; they don't have a nice word to say about the company; the management's rubbish; the training programmes are non-existent; they don't have enough tools and equipment… and so on. Whereas the most productive people, instead of bemoaning their lot and blaming a lack of resources, simply become incredibly resourceful: they find a way to bridge the gaps or they move on. I have regularly found when working with high-performing sports and business teams that the focus is always on resourcefulness. Here's a personal example of where I had to get resourceful when I started my business.

When I left my career with Gartner, which provided all the resources I needed to do my job, I started my own business in a pod office with a desk, laptop and telephone and I thought, am I crazy? I had no support, no customers, no brand, literally nothing. I thought, right, I've got to pay the bills in a month, what's the quickest way I can get off the ground and attract my first customers? My answer was to try to speak at local events, conferences and exhibitions to showcase my content and abilities. So, I rang up all the conferences in the UK saying, "Hi, my name's Martin Johnson, I'm a motivational speaker in leadership and management and I'm free to speak at your event" and the response was always the same:

"Yes, hi Martin, thanks for your call, can you send me a video of you speaking in front of 200 - 300 people or more and I'll consider you?" Deflated by these responses, I replied:

"Well I haven't got a video, if you put me on the stage I'll have a video…"

"Sorry Martin, we can't do that, please send us a video and we will consider you."

I rang every event and conference, small, medium and large in the UK, and no one would book me unless I could provide video evidence of me speaking in front of a large audience. At that point I'm thinking it's not happening for me. I didn't have the resources to attract the conference managers, so, I had to somehow create them.

I invested £10,000, created T2 Talks, convinced 200 people to come and sit in the audience and listen, invited four guest speakers to join me on stage and speak free of charge, and hired a professional film crew to capture and edit the footage into a highly professional package. All in a bid to give me my video, my resource, and half a chance of becoming a speaker, which would kick start my business. I had to get resourceful. Since then we've sold out multiple T2 Talks, reaching more than 1,000 people and have over 30,000 hits on YouTube.

So, next time you hit an issue, don't throw your hands up in despair - get resourceful. Refuse to become a victim of your environment and circumstances, look at what you have got and don't just focus on what you haven't. You may not be able to pull it off every time, but we all need the resilience and presence of mind to try.

Here's a useful exercise to help us when we feel at a loss. On a blank piece of paper draw a line down the middle and on the left hand side write Resources, on the right hand side write Resource-

We must become resourceful and look to exploit every opportunity

fulness. Now, under resources, write a list of all the things you have right now in your job or life that are at your disposal which could help you achieve what you want: equipment, staff, training, support, savings, whatever it might be... On the right hand side make a list of all the things you don't have, the lack of which frustrates you. Go on, run riot, open the floodgates.

Now, look at what you have written under resourcefulness and instead of blaming what you haven't got for your lack of progress, pick a few and start getting resourceful; the ones where, with a little thought and strategy, you can make progress towards what you really want. It may take some thinking time but it will be worth it and, I'm willing to bet, may even open up new and different opportunities for you. If you want to punch through walls, leap hurdles and overcome challenges, then you must start becoming resourceful.

Resources and Resourcefulness

1. Resources and resourcefulness are two entirely different things.

2. Draw a line down the middle of a piece of paper and make a list of everything you have to support your success and everything you don't have. Then start getting resourceful.

3. Resourcefulness is present in almost all successful and self-fulfilled people.

Mistake No 15:

The Ownership of Accountability

I have a frustration with some of today's business approaches, and one of them is the apparent need for shared responsibility, or more accurately, shared accountability. The notion that it's everyone's responsibility for this and that... This notion of sharing, of course, promotes inclusion, and it's a nice thought that we should all have a stake, share the burden and any success. But for me, in the majority of environments this approach becomes counterproductive because it actually leads to avoidance and a lack of accountability. And here's why:

The problem with a shared responsibility is that it's nobody's problem.

Nothing fuels productivity in our life, relationships or the workplace more than accountability. I get challenged on this statement a lot. In the business world, many CEOs and managers push back and argue that not everything should be assigned to an individual and that we should be able to have groups taking collective responsibility for something. But I hold firm, I insist that **we must not mistake accountability, or responsibility, for contribution**,. They are totally different things and we must be clear about them if we are going to get productive.

In the workplace, take strategy, vision, culture, health and safety, whatever it is, they all fundamentally rely on an individual to drive the agenda. For example, a company's culture cannot be everybody's responsibility – you don't agree? Here's the way I see it: of course everybody needs to contribute to influence an organisational culture. Everybody needs to adhere to and con- tribute to a good health and safety policy. Everybody, of course, is required to contribute to achieve a strategy or vision, but if you research the most successful, game-changing outcomes in histo- ry, they have all been owned and led by one significant individual.

Martin Luther King made it his responsibility to fight for Afri- can American human rights and end segregation in America. In turn, millions followed and contributed. Gandhi made it his life's mission to fight for Indian independence. Again, millions followed and contributed. Steve Jobs's dream was to make every human being on earth more productive through the use of technology. Millions bought in, followed and contributed. Those three out- standing, world-changing achievements happened because one person made it their responsibility, they took ownership of the is- sue and drove an outcome. Millions of others contributed to their success and followed their lead.

To come back to businesses now, I find that the most success- ful and clearly defined cultures are driven by one incredible indi- vidual. Usually the CEO, sometimes a board member, but always one person setting the tone and driving the agenda for everyone else to join in and contribute. When I visit businesses that paint their cultural values on the wall, claiming the workforce live and breathe them (presumably because they can read), it's often ap- parent that no one person is responsible for driving and delivering on those values. I find the workforce's understanding of the business's strategy and vision is patchy, the culture is weak and contribution is minimal.

Getting more specific, let's think about bins. You've got a big open office and it's everyone's responsibility to empty their own bin and recycle their rubbish every day. But if you don't make it part of one person's role to ensure that everyone does it, it tends not to happen. Bins will overflow. "Well, Dave never empties his bin, so why should I?" And then we have Bingate! People will start making up their own rules depending on how comfortable they are with mounting piles of rubbish. Some people won't care and others will be triggered into counterproductive behaviour because they can't cope with the mess. My point here is that when things are a shared responsibility, it tends to be no one's problem and it doesn't get done. An effective recycling policy, resupplying the stationery cupboard, locking up the office, making sure your client areas are welcoming and spotless – when it's someone's job it gets done. When it isn't, it doesn't.

In our personal lives it works the same way. Husbands, wives, partners, often both with careers, work hard and have children to look after too. The traditional stereotypes of homemaker and breadwinner are, thankfully, being consigned to history, and we now have more choice in how we want to organise our home lives. But the division of labour isn't easy. The most basic tasks set off arguments in the household, simply because there's no agreed ownership. Cleaning, walking the dog, insuring the car, cutting the lawn, the weekly shop, school trips, booking holidays... the list, as we all know, can feel endless. Yet when we agree who does what and take responsibility for it, we know where we stand and much of that stress and irritation (especially if you feel you do the lion's share) vanishes.

Ownership and accountability are really important both in our personal and working lives. If people aren't assigned ownership it becomes a shared responsibility, and the problem with a shared responsibility is that it is nobody's problem, which drives animosity, resentment and creates conflict.

If you want to change the world or just your world, start taking ownership, be accountable and mutually agree the things that others will become accountable for. Then lead by example and, in turn, you will encourage participation, collaboration and contribution from those around you.

"People may doubt what you say, but they'll always believe what you do."

Lewis Cass

The Ownership of Accountability

1. The problem with a shared responsibility is that it's nobody's problem!

2. We must not mistake accountability or responsibility for contribution.

3. In order to drive real change in our businesses and our lives, someone must take the responsibility to drive a change, and then inspire others around them to contribute - could that person be you?

Mistake No 16:
Fake It Till You Make It

"Fake it till you make it." When I make this statement I, understandably see raised eyebrows. Now, I am not advocating unethical behaviour or deceitful self-promotion. I'm saying that nothing is perfect, there is possibly never the right time nor the ideal set of circumstances, and in this sense you cannot wait an eternity before you throw yourself into something. Sometimes you just have to take a chance and seize the day!

> **"Ring the bells that still can ring**
> **Forget your perfect offering**
> **There is a crack in everything**
> **That's how the light gets in."**
> Leonard Cohen

In 2012 I watched a great TED talk on this subject by Amy Cuddy called, *Your Body Language May Shape Who You Are*[15]. It's up there with some of the most watched TED talks of all time and with good reason. It certainly hit home with me and it's where I first heard the phrase, "Fake it till you make it".

A social psychologist, Cuddy argues that presenting ourselves as confident and able, even if we feel less than ready, has far more to do with our success than we may imagine. It could even change our body chemistry.

At 19 I received a rarely presented Admiral's Commendation for my part in saving HMS Nottingham from sinking in the Tasman Sea[16]. This is one early example of me faking it. Here to tell the tale, thankfully, I did make it, along with the rest of the ship's company, in coming home alive. A young sailor and part of the Type 42 Destroyer crew, in 2002 we were deployed in the Far East for nine months and were sailing just off the coast of Lord Howe Island on our way to New Zealand. We had been at anchor most of the day in the bay with the Captain ashore, but as the sea state deteriorated, with rough weather approaching we decided to weigh anchor and head off early. Ten minutes after leaving our anchorage, I was thrown six feet across the mess deck by an almighty collision. As I discovered later, we had hit Wolf Rock, one of the largest rocks in the Tazman Sea, sitting just 6ft below the waterline. Water instantly poured in to the lower decks and we were 600 kms from anywhere that could offer help.

Investigations later found that the navigating officer was distracted with landing the ship's helicopter back on the flight deck, didn't have the sonar activated and had not taken time to properly plot our course and speed. He realised his mistake too late to stop us being cut open like a can of beans, ripping a 49-metre hole from bow to bridge. We were literally stuck on this rock and the noise was horrifying. As part of the emergency party, I raced to my muster station. Standing beside white-faced, experienced sailors, we were all scared, yet I put my hand up and volunteered to go down into the ship's compartments and seal the hatches to stop the water coming in further. Waist-deep in rising water, was I terrified? Yes. Did I have the confidence I was displaying? No. Was I going to let it stop me? No. I, along with half a dozen others, entered the compartments, sealed the hatches and we managed to stabilise the ship. Since that day, and confirmed in Amy Cuddy's TED talk and countless other less dramatic moments in my life, I know that my confidence and body language have been key factors in my productivity. Because sometimes you have to fake it until you make it. Here's another short example.

After leaving the Royal Navy I went for an interview with Butler Group, a small consulting company. They required a minimum of five years' IT or technology and sales experience for new recruits. I went into the first interview, I gave them the big sell about the Navy, my social experience and strong communication skills, and they were impressed but wanted more detail on my technical experience. I told them about the operations room and weapon systems, how I used to be involved getting them back online when they went down… Now, there was, without doubt, an element of truth in that… Element being the word! I was staying factual but still not underselling myself. I needed that job and was faking it to try and make it. I got the job.

Three days into the role and I was talking with senior IT professionals about computers and servers with no clue. I decided I had to come clean with my manager, said that I didn't really know that much about IT and was struggling with the terminology. Thankfully he laughed and said not to worry: he made sure I learnt the ropes and within 12 months I was promoted to team leader.

In my early career I used the same technique with my public speaking. Through practice and perseverance, I now genuinely love speaking to audiences and have a wealth of experience to draw upon. In the beginning, I was ill-prepared and terrified, but it didn't deter me.

There are moments in life when you just can't wait for perfection. Sometimes it's about taking a calculated risk and it's thought that the influence of our body language on others is as high as 65% of our overall impact. It also acts positively on our own inner confidence. As I said earlier in the book, we cannot control people's thoughts but we can influence their thinking. At times you have to fake it until you make it. You have to display a level of external confidence and competency and by doing so, grow it internally as well.

If I had frozen when the ship hit the rock, others would have frozen.
If I'd displayed anxiety when speaking in public, the audience would have become anxious.
If I'd told my employer I had no clue about technology, I wouldn't have got the job.

Fake it till you make it. Why not? Pick your moment and push your chest out. All the most wealthy, senior and successful people do!

Fake It Till You Make It

1. We cannot wait for perfection until we throw ourselves in and have a go.

2. Our body language and how we portray ourselves can be up to 65% of our influence.

3. Remember: people's perceptions of us are almost fully based on our behaviours and traits. So, if in doubt, 'Fake It Till You Make It'. Most other people are.

Mistake No 17:
Forming Highly Productive Habits

When I talk to individuals, teams and even entire conferences about this, I play a simple but highly effective visual game. I produce a tennis ball on stage and ask everyone to clap once when they think the ball is going to bounce - timing their clap to coincide with the ball hitting the floor. If they don't clap when the ball is bounced, they're out. I do this nice and slowly and everyone usually gets the hang of it and claps when the ball hits the floor. Then I speed it up a bit. Bounce after bounce, everyone is clapping. Everyone is doing great and we're all rather pleased with ourselves. I speed the game up a little more and when everyone is in a rhythm, unexpectedly, I hang on to the ball. There is no bounce BUT, without fail, everyone claps, everyone is out and the game is over.

The reason this works as a great illustration of an idea is because I can quickly instill a habit or learned behaviour in you, by you clapping when my ball bounces. And in the same moment I can demonstrate how that quickly learned but unconscious habit can let you down when I stop the bounce but you still clap – you get caught out in record time! Human beings are highly adaptable, we learn fast and can form habits just as quickly. Knowing this, we need to regularly review or challenge these habits as our environment or situation changes. But why do we humans form habits?

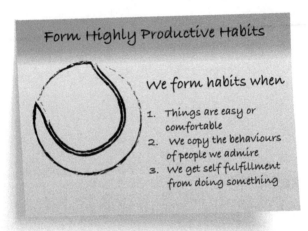

Firstly, we like doing things that are easy or comfortable. Watching the TV instead of going for a run. Putting off that report or piece of work until tomorrow because we can't be bothered right now. When things are easy or comfortable we tend to want to do them over and over because it doesn't give us any stress.

Secondly, our human tendency to copy and replicate others' behaviour. We learn from significant people in our lives, those we admire or just spend the majority of our time with. Gossiping is a classic example; we can get dragged into that kind of behaviour if we spend a lot of time with someone who is always talking about other people's business. We also pick up turns of phrase that our partners or colleagues use.

Thirdly, we formulate habits from doing the things that bring us genuine self-fulfilment. When we get self-fulfilment, our brains release dopamine, which makes us feel happy and content. We are engaged, we get a 'buzz' and we want to replicate the action time and time again.

Going back to the tennis ball for a moment. When we learn the rules and begin slowly, we feel good, we gain confidence as the ball hits the ground faster and we are right on it. We are finding it easy but, suddenly without realising it, we are on autopilot. We are not watching closely, the situation changes, the ball doesn't hit the floor and we get caught out. If we want to be productive we have to constantly sense check and challenge our habits. Are they working for us or against us? Because the minute something in our circumstances or environment shifts, we will make a mistake. We need to think about refining the habits we have, or adopting new ones, to drive the kind of results we are looking for.

Early on in my business we formed a habit. Our working hours were set at nine to five. As many, many businesses adopt the nine to five working day, why should we be any different? We'd instantly formed a habit copied from other business models without too much thought or reasoning. Now, as with most cities, in Hull where my business is based, there are two peak times for traffic during the day. In order to get in on time, staff were setting off incredibly early to have a half decent journey in, even arriving an hour early just to ensure they didn't have the stress of the rush hour and worrying that they wouldn't make it by nine o'clock. This had a powerful effect on our productivity and contentment as a team. I discovered that people who had been in since eight o'clock were not really working up to five. They were packing up and watching the clock from around half past four, fretting about the state of the congestion and how long it may take them to get home, and I was doing exactly the same thing. So I started to alter my behaviour.

The difference between me setting off for home at four o'clock was a 20-minute journey, as opposed to an hour's journey if I set off at five o'clock. I found myself creeping off a bit early every day. I am the CEO, so I could. But, guess what? My team began to copy my newly-formed habit and reasons to get away themselves. It was a negative process that meant we actually weren't getting a full day's work in: we were all focused on the clock more than what needed to be finished.

The habit we had formed wasn't working. It was a learnt, copied behaviour that was, for us, becoming counterproductive. So I challenged this habit and changed the rules. I brought in a new habit. I said that all the team could begin their working day at eight or eight-thirty and finish at four or four-thirty, whichever suited them and their journey times. I empowered them to choose. The real focus was to be on putting in a full day's work. No clock watching, no time wasting. Meanwhile they could make their daily commute as efficient as possible. Since that moment, our productivity has gone through the roof. No one is late, because they have the ownership and accountability over their start and finish time, and everyone remains productive right up until the moment they have chosen to leave for the day.

Thirty minutes. That's all it took to change our whole outlook, and wrapped up in the new habit is a little bit of empowerment for the team to choose their hours of arrival and when they finish. This also touches on business culture from Chapter 15 and how one person needs to be responsible for driving it. If I hadn't felt accountable for our business culture and how this particular issue was negatively impacting us, would anyone have bothered to address it? I doubt it, it wasn't their responsibility.

And here's the key point I want to make. Ultimately, the third reason for forming habits, that of self-fulfilment, should be our focus. Finding self-fulfilment in our home and work lives is really what it's all about. In the hobbies we take up, in our exercise regimes and the careers we pursue. Sales for me is a job that comes with a real buzz, doing the deal, closing the business, overcoming challenges, and I get genuine self-fulfilment and want to replicate that feeling again and again. It's the same for the barrister who wins their case; the writer who finishes their book; the hotelier who's getting five-star reviews. If you put this book down now and analysed your habits, how many exist because they are easy? Which are the ones that you've picked up or learned from others? Scrutinise how these are working for you and make some changes. Focus on the habits which bring you genuine self-fulfilment. Do the things you enjoy. Get off the sofa, stop following the herd and do what makes you happy and fulfilled, as this is when you'll be at your most productive.

Forming Highly Productive Habits

1. We humans form habits for three reasons: when something is easy, a learnt or copied behaviour, and when we get self-fulfilment from doing something.

2. The first two reasons don't always result in productive habits and we must challenge them.

3. If we focus on forming the habits that give us genuine self-fulfilment, we are likely to become very productive in our efforts.

Mistake No 18:
Increase Your Resilience

I talked earlier in the book of how, as a species, we have lost some of our resilience. Early in our evolution we were among the most resilient species on the planet, moving up the food chain, evading predators, using our cognitive brain to make tools, hunt, create fire and survive at all costs. Today, with heat, water, light and food on tap, advances in medicine and security, our safety (thankfully near-death experiences are extremely rare) is pretty much guaranteed. But the technology we have at our fingertips and the media we are exposed to 24/7 have significantly skewed our perception of reality. Also, remember in Chapter six when we looked at how our education system views failure and our per-ceived 'lack' of success in a highly consumer-driven society can make us dissatisfied, depressed even? Well, it's time to wrestle back some control.

We have to keep knocking…

After joining the Butler Group with my "Fake it till you make it" approach, I got excited about my career development and wanted to move to a company that could offer me more scope. I did my research and began focusing on global leader, Gartner. At the time, Gartner was a £1 billion global IT advisory and consultancy firm based in Stamford in the US. I was with a UK-based £12 million start-up, a great company, but I felt I had served my apprenticeship and I was ready for something more challenging.

I was around 24 years old and, as a competitor of mine, I knew a little bit about Gartner. I watched what they did and how they did it. I really admired their culture and the resources they commanded. I wanted to work for them. I looked up their senior HR Partner in the UK, a guy called Simon Marus. I'll never forget Simon. Through LinkedIn I found his phone number and called him.

"Hi Simon, my name's Martin, you don't know me. I'm a guy from Hull, I'm a top salesman at a competitor of yours, I sell what you sell and I want to come and work for you."

"Right, Martin, thank you for the call, send me your CV and we'll keep you on file." I felt a bit deflated. I sent him my CV and heard nothing back, so a week later…

"Hi Simon, it's Martin again, I've had a great sales month you know and I'm still the top salesman and I could be this for Gartner, I want to work for you, I want to work for the global brand, the global leaders."

"Well, absolutely Martin, as I said last time, we don't have any roles open in the north of England as yet, but we'll keep you on file and we know where you are, thanks for your interest."

And this went on. I emailed Simon month after month and I messaged him at every opportunity. Every time I closed a big deal I sent him an email, every time he posted something on LinkedIn I commented. I was literally stalking the man and I just kept knocking and, here's the thing when you keep knocking, after a while you can't be ignored. Every month, "Hi Simon, It's Martin again, any roles in the north?"

"Not yet Martin but I appreciate your tenacity."

"Hi Simon, It's Martin". And the other problem when you keep doing this is that gets annoying, so in the end he said:

"Martin, listen, right, here's the deal. I'm up in Manchester, I'll meet you at Manchester Service Station. I cannot promise anything but I will meet you, I will meet you for an hour."

"It's a deal!" I said.

I went to Manchester Service Station and had an hour's conversation with Simon and one of the hiring managers, Victoria Farmer. I spent one hour trying to convince them of why I should have an opportunity, and why they could employ me as a remote-based worker in the north of England. How I could win new business clients, I'd start from scratch and make my own territory. I said if there's wasn't a role available I would create one for myself, just give me the shot. Simon's response was, "Yes, Martin, I love what I hear but you're a bit green, you're 24, 25... For a senior field role in Gartner, we don't usually, you know, hire people without five or ten years' experience in the sector."

"Yes, I know Simon but I can sell. Look, you're here!"

He laughed, "Right, I'll tell you what, I'll do you a deal, you come down to Egham in Surrey and we'll put you through a panel interview, it'll be in front of the Regional Vice President and some of the key stakeholders in a room, you've got 15 minutes to tell us why you? Why should we hire you? We'll have a vote around the room. If it's a unanimous vote you get an opportunity, if not, you're going to have to leave me alone."

"Deal, that's all I want Simon, thank you."

So, down I went to Egham. I prepared a presentation about my background and why I had a deep-seated, burning sense of purpose. Boy, did I deliver that presentation with passion and belief. I did my 15 minutes and they asked me to leave the room.

Five minutes later they asked me back into the room. It was a unanimous vote, I got the job at 24 years old. It took me probably six months of emailing, calling and sending my CV. I wasn't aggressive, I was trying to do it in an endearing and thoughtful way, but all the same I kept knocking. I landed at Gartner and my career took off. Within a short period of time I was a sales leader with a $5 million territory, from which I set up my own company, became a keynote speaker and now, today, am writing this book. I chose to keep knocking. Remember the Beatles and JK Rowling? Listen to constructive criticism, listen to what people are telling you BUT, if you feel in your gut you've got what it takes, accept early rejection as part and parcel of life and just keep going.

Biding their time... Chinese bamboo trees.

Patience is a virtue.

The second story I'm going to use to illustrate this point is very short, but it's a favourite of mine. You may have come across it before. It's true and it really resonates with me, it's the story of the Chinese bamboo tree.

Now, the Chinese bamboo tree is quite an incredible thing. When you sow the seed in the ground it takes five years' care and attention, feeding and watering before the first shoots break through the soil. Five years before you'll see any results of your patient nurturing. But, here's the thing. Within five weeks of the first shoots breaking through the soil, the Chinese bamboo tree grows to around 90 feet tall. How extraordinary is that?

For me this reflects many aspects of life. How can we bring a project or an idea to fruition and work away to achieve our goals without patience, determination and resilience? People observing a lack of progress may think we're nuts and advise us to give up. We think we're going nuts, as nothing appears to be coming from all of our hard work. I speak to so many people who have given up on starting that business or chasing that recruiter, keeping up with their personal training programme or fighting for their department. They give up because they don't see immediate results, they don't see instant progress and effectively they give up on themselves. Well, we need to have more resilience. We need to understand that real change takes time, and that sticking to our values and beliefs is important and will bring us the outcomes we want, including new and different opportunities.

When we watch our children and our close friends, we can see their natural abilities and how that shapes their lives; how some things come easily to one child but not to the other. Who struggles, who makes a leap ahead. Who has natural determination and a will to succeed despite the odds. Whatever our talents, to understand that patience and resilience are an important part of who we become is a hugely valuable lesson to learn – and the earlier the better!

To build greater resilience we must keep knocking, allow ourselves a little failure but keep positive in our thoughts. It also means we accept that it will take time and that we must be patient. In a world where we can buy goods with a credit card and the click of a button and they are on our doorstep the next day, we need to remind ourselves that if we want something of true value we will have to go and find it, or even create it. We have to give it some time and we mustn't give up on our goal or ourselves. We must develop a level of resillience in both ourselves and our children.

Increase Your Resilience

1. We have gone from the most resilient species on earth to arguably the most anxious. Well, it's time to wrestle some control.

2. Keep knocking - remember the Chinese bamboo tree. Don't give up, ever!

3. Patience - if we want something of true value we will have to go find it or create it, and we must give it time.

Mistake No 19:
The Power of Three

My fascination with human behaviour over the past 14 years, includes how we, as humans, get things done, and, more importantly, the best and most productive way to do them. What's very apparent is that we are not effective if we try to do more than three things at a time. Now, the key word here is perhaps not 'three' but 'effective'. Many of us claim to multi-task but the quality of our work takes a significant dive when we are asked to juggle more than three things. More than this, if we do only have three things to focus on, we should be only be focused on ONE at any given moment.

To illustrate this, here's a great little test which I first read about in *Psychology Today* from The Potential Group based in Denmark. Have a go yourself and you'll quickly see what I mean.

On a piece of paper draw two lines horizontally across the page. On the first line write down, "I am a great multi-tasker". On the second line write down the numbers one to 20. Time how long it takes you to write out each line and make a note.

I am a great multi-tasker
1 2 3 4 5 6 7 8 9 10 11 12 13 14 15 16 17 18 19 20

On average, the top line will have taken you about five seconds to write. The second line will have taken around eight or nine seconds to write down.

Now, draw two more horizontal lines below these across the page. This time write down the same things on your two lines BUT you are going to alternate between writing the first letter of the statement and the first number in the sequence, then the second letter, then the second number, and carry on until you have completed both the statement and the sequence of numbers. In other words, write 'I' then '1', write 'a' then '2', write 'm' then '3' etc.… Set a timer on your phone to see how long it takes you. When you're done, check the timings and have a think about these questions:

1. **How much longer did it take?**

2. **Did you leave any spaces between the words?**

3. **What does your handwriting look like?**

From this simple exercise we can demonstrate that we cannot focus on two things **effectively** in one moment. If we try to multi-task, for example by being on the phone whilst typing up an email and writing a report, the quality of our work will significantly drop and the time it takes to complete any of the given tasks will rise. We can also tip ourselves into a sense of building anxiety, like that octopus on roller skates – we're not being as effective or productive as we could be.

We work at our most productive when we limit our focus to three things at any time and focus on only one of those in any given moment.

You can easily see that during our daily lives, as we shop, while on the phone and telling off an awkward child, we are not focused, we are not present, we'll miss things and we'll make mistakes. Look back at the written task. The harder it got, the more scruffy our handwriting was, we're trying to stay on task but our brain is hurting and we're in survival mode just to get it completed. Neuroscience also backs up what happens when we take the test.

Recent research suggests that our brains don't, or more specifically can't, do two things at once, as many people believe. When we think we are doing two or more things at once, our brains are actually switching between the tasks, albeit it very, very quickly. And this 'stop-start' brain function means that we're working much harder than we need to - it's rough on our brains, it saps our energy, we make more mistakes, we feel more stressed – here comes that octopus again…

To get a handle on our busy lives and make them more productive and more enjoyable, let's forget the idea that we should attempt, let alone admire, multi-tasking. It's a seductive myth. Instead, we need to focus on three things in our lives. For me at this moment my focus is the health and wellbeing of my family, growing my business and writing this book. That's it. This morning, before I left the house, I am focused on my family, I give all my energy to them, they have my full attention. Arriving at work, I am fully focused on what I need to achieve that day and how I am supporting my team. Within that day I block out three hours to work with my editor, Jacky. During those three hours I'm not thinking about either my family or my business: I'm fully focused on trying to get my ideas down on paper and I need to get it right because I don't want to shortchange you with my life's work! I will give myself the best chance of meeting the needs of my family, my business and my book (and retain my sanity) if I focus on one, and only one, at any given moment.

The power of three also crops up in other places. When I coach people for speaking and presenting, a great rule of thumb is an introduction, three salient points and a wrap-up. Our minds can comfortably absorb and retain three salient points. You'll notice in this book that I try to keep my points to three or less for each chapter, so that they are easy for you to absorb and retain. I am willing to bet that you can remember three things easily on a list, yet when it stretches to four it becomes appreciably harder. On a night out I also always think that it's a good idea to have three beers and go home. I'm still working on that but think how many problems that would solve?!

Think about your current focus. Try to adopt the power of three, as it will allow you to focus on the things that you can both control and gain self-fulfilment from. Most importantly, it will allow you to do them extremely well.

The Power of Three

1. We can only focus effectively on three things at any one time, and on one thing in any given moment.

2. Feeling like the octopus on roller skates? If so, make a change.

3. Multi-tasking significantly reduces our ability to perform tasks and activities effectively.

Mistake No 20:
Fail Fast and Move On

Earlier in the book I talked about our current education system which, more often than not, reinforces the notion that failure is always bad, and how that skews our perception of ourselves and the world around us. In reality, failure is a natural part of learning and we need to allow ourselves a little room for failure. This chapter is going to look at that idea in a bit more depth in that, yes, it's important to allow ourselves to fail BUT it's just as important to be able to move on and move on fast.

Bounce-back-ability, if it's a word at all, is probably the perfect word to use here. It's the knack of getting up and getting on. Some of us have this naturally; an ability to throw ourselves into a project and, if it doesn't pan out, we're OK with that. We dust ourselves down and look around for the next opportunity. Many leaders whom I meet foster a success-only environment, so, if you imagine (or maybe you don't have to) coming out of school with this fear of failure and entering the world of work where the

FAILURE IS NOT THE OPPOSITE OF SUCCESS IT IS PART OF SUCCESS

same values are played out, makes for a fearful work environment where people want to avoid failure at all cost. If we want to encourage innovation and greater productivity, the fail-fast-and-move-on principle needs to be adopted and encouraged far more within leadership teams and across organisations. It's about fostering an environment that supports people, makes them feel safe, empowers and enables them to think and talk about new ideas, new processes, take on new projects and learn from them.

When I challenge board executives and directors on this issue, I often meet with a wall of silence. When we dig down to find out why this presents such an issue, I find that they are so governed by their own metrics and required outcomes that they end up pressuring their managers, who in turn pressure their teams, the leaders of which put the fear of God into individuals and there is little or no room for learning - for people to fail fast and move on. And this behaviour is hampering the progress of many businesses across the globe. Without a shadow of a doubt, the most productive people I come across are those who are not afraid to try; to fail fast, learn lessons and move on. So, if businesses do want to improve productivity they must foster an environment where people are allowed to experiment and fail.

This, of course comes with some caveats... health and safety cannot be compromised, you can't set young apprentices working on complex machinery and apply the fail fast and move on principle, they may end up moving on with fewer fingers! I get it, there are some non-negotiables and that's perfectly right, but where can they fail? It's well worth the leadership team coming together and identifying what's operationally critical or non-negotiable, and other areas where employees can be innovative and creative. That's where our most productive people shine and their innovation can and will supercharge business growth.

Fail Fast and Move On

1. Those of us who foster a fail-fast-and-move-on mentality produce some of the most creative environments.

2. In order to do this we must decide on our negotiables and non-negotiables. Where is it safe for people to innovate and try new things?

3. If all we do is reprimand mistakes and inaccuracies within our businesses and homes, we will create a fearful 'must not fail' culture

Mistake No 21:

Set Audacious But Achievable Goals

There has been a lot written about setting goals. It's an undeniable fact that as humans in life and in business without goals, a vision, an end game, call it what you like, without an idea of the outcome you want to achieve, getting there is nigh on impossible. But to understand goals, I believe you must first understand the Law of Attraction.

There's a book that splits opinion on this called *The Secret*, a best-selling 2006 self-help book by Rhonda Byrne[16]. The book is based on the premise that if you 'think' it, it will happen. Byrne brings in quotes from philosophers and thought leaders and her content goes on to touch on spirituality. Now, I'm not at all sure about 'talking' to the universe (if you do, no problem, you're perfectly entitled), but within the ideas Byrne puts forward there seems to me plenty of common sense, namely:

**If we think positively and drive positive thoughts, we'll
experience positive outcomes and rewards in life.
If we think negatively, are pessimistic and constantly hold
back for fear of failure, we'll experience more negativity,
poorer outcomes and less opportunity in life.**

Unlike Rhonda, my belief is that our positive and negative think-ing releases those brain chemicals that we looked at earlier in the book; we're either in survival mode when cortisol is impacting our thought processes, or possibly dopamine when we're loving what we're doing and motivated to do more. However, I do agree that the Law of Attraction becomes really powerful when it involves creating a vision and setting goals. When we set ourselves goals and visualise the outcome we are far more likely to succeed, so why not set audacious ones? For me that's the real value of the Law of Attraction. I've been doing it all my life and it has a big part to play in the things I have achieved to date.

The Hollywood star Jim Carey tells a great story about the Law of Attraction in relation to goal setting... Oprah Winfrey was in-terviewing him and they touched on the time before he was a highly paid movie star. He went on to share the story of when he sat down and wrote himself a cheque for $10 million and the power of that single action, thought and the vision that he creat-ed around it. Even though we may think, oh, it's a crazy, material-istic thing to do, it signalled his intent. It was audacious. It was his goal. He kept that dummy cheque. It represented the status he wanted professionally, the financial freedom and artistic recogni-tion. And look at the outcome. We all know that it was realistic, he got there and is, in all likelihood, paid much more than $10 million for a movie today.

Another example, this time from sport: Roger Bannister was determined that he could run a four-minute mile. At the time no one thought it was humanly possibly to run that distance at that speed. But Bannister set his goal, visualising himself crossing the finishing line and breaking the record. He put in milestones to reach this goal and at every stage visualised reaching and passing those milestones. He knew his ultimate goal may be audacious, so he put in realistic stepping stones, or milestones, in order for him to get there and he did. Since that day more than 1,000 people, including a high school student and a 40-year-old adult, have run a sub four-minute mile because when that barrier was broken by Bannister, it suddenly became a reality for others. But it took Bannister's vision, his positive belief and determination for it to happen in the first place.

Goal setting and visualisation is an immensely powerful tool. I use it in everything I do. Recently, I worked with a professional sports team and deployed these techniques. I wanted the players to visualise the match coming up and I wanted them to imagine in their beds at night or over a coffee during the week everything they were going to do in that game; from scoring points to executing plays and communicating well with their fellow team mates. I wanted them to think about and use mental imagery to imagine themselves scoring the winning point for the team in the last minute and the crowd going absolutely crazy. I wanted them to use that imagery to create the law of attraction. And, once we'd done that for a period of time, I changed it up slightly.

Now, the Law of Attraction states that we shouldn't think negative thoughts but, to make them more resilient during a game, I wanted the pro players to visualise things going wrong in the first ten minutes, then visualise how they would react to this in a positive way and recover. Because, if all we do is use imagery for positive scenarios, when it comes to our mistakes, knock-backs and obstacles we can easily get blown off course. This approach enabled many of them to anticipate and deal with any early controversy in a game, keep their heads up and build the positive energy needed to stay focused.

A taboo subject for goal setting appears to be around money and financial reward. Think back to Jim Carey and what your initial thoughts may have been around him writing out that cheque. I firmly believe that there is nothing wrong with setting financial goals and being motivated by the achievement of wealth. We live in a world where a certain level of wealth is necessary for ourselves and our families' wellbeing. In most cases we can only have time and freedom if we have first of all paid the bills. If we want choice, we need financial freedom. To gain freedom, we need to set ourselves financial goals.

I have often noticed that people set their financial goals not just around earning but also saving and managing their money. I am one of the few who sets my goals purely around making money. It's an entirely different approach and thought process, and I want to share it with you.

For the years I have left in my professional career, I'm not setting goals around earning enough to pay my bills and saving something to help my children. I am focused on goals that will make me more money and ensure my financial freedom.

So what's your financial mindset? Are you trying to make enough to survive, save and manage, or are you trying to expand your horizons, open up new opportunities and make as much money as you can?

The Money Mindset

When it comes to setting your goals, you should not be ashamed or coy about including financial and money-related objectives. This is what some of the most successful and self-fulfilled entrepreneurs do. You may have heard the saying:

"For the love of money is the route of all evil…"
1 Timothy 6:10 The Bible.

This text is often misquoted as, "Money is the route of all evil". What is less well-known is the complete text:

"For the love of money is the route of all evil, eager for
money, people have wandered from the faith and pierced
themselves with many griefs."

The complete version is not saying that money alone is the issue, but that our love of and greed for money could well be.

Given the regular misquoting of the verse, we are all brought up to think that being motivated by money is distasteful, shallow and greedy. Let's face it, there are many, many instances of money becoming the monster, but there are also plenty of examples of money creating health, wealth and happiness. Whatever your view, all I ask is that you keep an open mind as you read the next section. This is my view on setting effective financial goals and the importance of them.

Money the monster
Money has funded conflict and war
Money has fuelled crime
Money creates envy and greed
Money can distort our values and morals
Money dictates our standard of living, health and wellbeing

Money the enabler
Money motivates innovation and invention
Money is instrumental in trading and human collaboration
Money fuelled the scientific, medical and technological revolution
Money drove the Industrial Revolution

Whether you agree with the idea of money as a system of exchange or not, it's not money itself that dictates these outcomes, it's humans - it's us.

Money: how we choose to view it and use it

We need a healthy relationship with money. We need to understand that it's the system we have, it's not going away. Through our action, it has the ability to harm or enable us. We have to choose enable and to do this we need to understand the two modern mindsets when it comes to money.

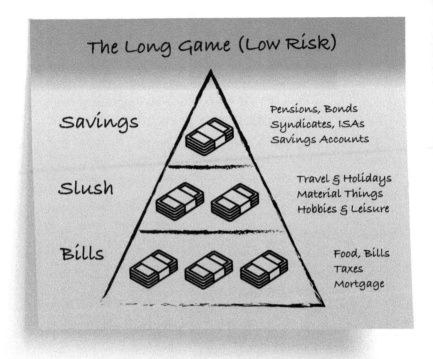

The Long Game

The Long Game is the money-saving mindset. Most of us are aware of this and it's a mindset that has been passed down from generation to generation. We work hard, develop a single solid income, pay our bills, pay our taxes, leaving ourselves a weekly or monthly slush fund. If we're lucky enough to have some left over, it gets put away for a rainy day. This model is based on a consistent and guaranteed income, careful budgeting and an eye on safeguarding the future.

In my experience of this type of money management mindset, the bottom level, the 'bills', is always the biggest section by monetary amount. The second level, the 'slush', is a smaller amount. The third level, the 'savings', is always the smallest amount and tends to be added to only when we can afford it. If we are highly disciplined people on a guaranteed income, 'The Long Game' will pay off for us.

This mindset served me well for a time and it works for many people who live within their means and manage their money carefully. They are happy and content and who are we to judge? The problem with 'The Long Game' is that life gets in the way, income is not as consistent as we would like and very few of us are disciplined enough to make it pay off.

Let's look now at my mindset towards money and that of almost all the entrepreneurs I meet.

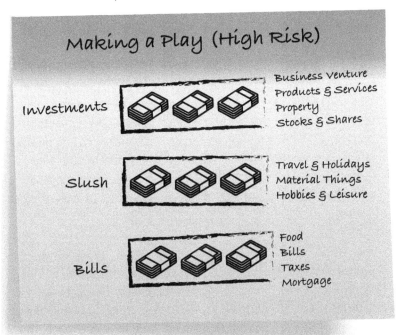

Making a Play

Making a Play is my mindset today because I want to be financially free by the time I am 45 years old. I want to be in a position to use money as an enabler for myself, my family and others, while I still have the energy and health to make a difference. The only way I can achieve this is by flipping The Long Game on its head and generating as much money as I can, as fast as I can. All of my personal and professional goals have a financial sum attached to them. I can see it. I can visualise it and, in my mind, nothing is going to stop me.

Making a Play is not a money-saving mindset, it's a money-making mindset. I still have to pay the bills. I still need a slush fund; however, the difference with this mindset is that for every single penny I have left over, I don't tuck it away in the bank or building society, I re-invest it in something that will generate more money.

My wife will tell you that I never used to think like this. I was always playing The Long Game. I was never happy unless I had a good amount in our savings account. She would say to me "Loosen up, you're a long time dead!" But then, around three years ago, something changed my point of view. I woke up one day and decided that I didn't want to play The Long Game any more. Within four weeks I had handed in my notice at Gartner, the company I had fought hard to get into and which had given me lots of opportunity and resources. Three months after that I had registered Trans2 Performance and secured my first portfolio of clients. That was the start of my new mindset. I was Making my Play.

For the first two levels, Making a Play mindset is the same as The Long Game, but I noticed that entrepreneurs and goal-driven people almost always have a greater slush fund fed by multiple income feeds, which leads into the all-important level three. Instead of it being about saving money, it's all about generating it. Turning money into more money, looking for new opportunities and reinvestment. Without doubt this approach has higher risk factors and is harder to set up. But, once it begins to bear fruit, an entire world of opportunities opens up and that freedom you're looking for comes a little closer.

I had gone from a solid career income, my bills paid, a generous slush fund, even a pension pot and some savings tucked away. Life was OK. I switched it and made my play. In the last three years, as well as writing this book, I have set up a business with multiple product and service lines, generated four streams of income and plan to add two more in the next twelve months.

To achieve this I had to take many risks; calculated, yes, but risks nonetheless, and that is the part that prevents many people from moving out of The Long Game mindset. They're trapped. Part of my risk was giving up my job. Lowering my guaranteed income to the bare minimum, emptying my slush fund and living off or investing every extra penny I had. Remember the Fake It Till You Make It chapter and my video investment? Today I generate revenue through my training business, events business, public speaking engagements and as an author. I am also set to launch a technology product shortly. Here's the thing though, many people told me that I was crazy. They told me:

"You can't run a business!"

"You can't write a book!"

"You can't stand up in front of 500 people and speak!"

The reality is that the people who told me this are trapped in The Long Game. They have set their own limitations and limited their own possibilities along with an enhanced fear of risk. Well, I don't play that game any more, so thank you for your concern, it's touching, but move aside I'm on a mission here…

People say, "Money goes to money."
Rubbish!
I say,
Money goes to people who are good with money.

With the exception of an inheritance, I can tell you that money generally goes to people who Make a Play. Even a lottery winner had to take a gamble and buy their ticket. You've got to be in it to win it, right? So, you have your two money mindset options. You can play The Long Game or you can Make a Play. There is no right or wrong, it's what works for you. **But beware!** Many people in our modern world are adopting The Long Game mindset, while living far beyond their means. They have debt, their credit cards are maxed; mortgages they can't afford; personal payment plans for the new car; they live with worry and they struggle. They may have The Long Game mindset but they have a Make a Play life-style. The two don't mix. If this is you, all you have to do is either discipline yourself to live within your means or, go all in and make your play.

Many people set up businesses that fail. Many dabble in investments and they fail; many have a little 'side' business that fails. The businesses often fail because there's a safety net, the owners didn't go all in. It's like the well-known life coach and author Tony Robbins[18] once famously said: "If you want to take the island, then you must burn your boats." When humans go all in on an endeavour and have no other option but to succeed, by and large, they tend to succeed.

So, what are you?
A money saver or a money maker?

Finally, to round off this chapter let's recap on how we can benefit from goal setting. I'm sure you've heard of Big Hairy Audacious Goals (BHAGs), right? They're great to motivate you but I would add that we must also make them ACHIEVABLE. Add in those milestone goals and visualise the steps, just like Banister running the mile and Carey's rise to Hollywood royalty.

1. **Make your goals exciting, but also slightly daunting.**

   "Shoot for the moon. Even if you miss, you'll land amongst the stars."
   Norman Vincent Peale

1. **Make them public.** It makes you accountable and far more likely to carry them through.

2. **Prepare for negativity.** Get ready for criticism - it always arrives! Most of the time it's not personal.

3. **Decide on your sacrifices.** You will have to go without to get ahead, but don't let it be your loved ones or inner circle. They cannot be replaced but just about everything else can be.

4. **Give it a deadline.** Even if it is far off, put in the milestones and give them a deadline so that you can chart your progress and push hard when you need to. Maybe, just maybe, it is your time to make a play.

Set Audacious Goals

1. Goal setting is an incredibly powerful thing. It creates the 'Law of Attraction'

2. Make them audacious and scary, but realistic

3. Don't be afraid to incorporate financial goals. Are you playing The Long Game or are you Making a Play?

Mistake No 22:
The Power of Repetition

Thinking back to earlier in the book, I looked at our worst fears and how restricting they can be on our lives. How crazy it was that public speaking is most people's worst fear, worse even than dying! This is where the power of repetition can really help, because repeating something over and over again is the single most effective way of overcoming a fear. And not just overcoming a fear, but also mastering a craft. They say "practice makes perfect" but practice doesn't actually make perfect as nothing is ever perfect – but it makes you bloody good.

It is human nature to try and to avoid something that we fear, or something that is difficult and takes a great deal of effort. Our brains release cortisol as we become anxious, then our sense of relief by avoiding the experience is stored away in our brains to be wheeled out the next time we are confronted with the same situation or task. In doing this we are basically reinforcing our fears, and the next time we encounter something similar our anxiety will be more severe and our desire for relief more pressing, and so on. For example, if you are afraid of heights and you've never crossed a bridge, climbed a ladder or looked over a balcony, your fear of heights, any heights, will become crippling. But if we face this head on and climb stairs, look out of windows, cross bridges, even with a fear of heights, this repetition will help us contain our anxiety and start to reduce and manage the impact.

It took me three attempts to pass my driving test (not my finest hour!) I remember driving the tests in sheer terror. Terror of making a mistake, stalling, crashing… I recall the first moment after I'd passed and I am sitting in a car without my instructor and I thought to myself, I can't drive a car, I only just scraped through the test third time! I was anxious to say the least. Fast-forward to today and I've been driving for many years, and now I do it with ease. We don't hang on to the initial terror because when we repeat the task time and again, it starts to feel completely natural.

Why is it then that we don't repeat the driving test analogy for everything else in life that makes us feel uneasy or fearful? If we don't like spiders, we run away from them. If we are scared of heights, we avoid going up tall things and fear getting on aeroplanes. If we are scared of public speaking we avoid it like the plague… and in turn our fear grows. If we followed the driving test principle we would be handling spiders, scaling tall buildings and speaking comfortably in public.

Another example from professional sport. Again, when I was working with a particular team, one of the players was having a tough time catching the ball. He'd been catching balls since he knew what a ball was, but, due to making some highly public fumbles in front of 20,000 people, his natural 'autopilot' ability to judge and catch a ball had been replaced in his mind with an ugly little 'gremlin'. These terms again come from Steve Peters's book *The Chimp Paradox*[19]. Peters explains that the 'autopilot' and the 'gremlin' are used by our brains to capture different experiences. This player had been on auto-pilot catching the ball skillfully for years. Five poor performances later, a lack of confidence crept in and all he could think about was NOT dropping the ball and what did he do? He kept dropping it. It became a real mental block for him and he asked for my help. "Now, there's no silver bullet for this kind of thing" I said. "But here's what I want you to do. Stay behind after training and catch 100 balls every day before the next big game." Despite being puzzled that the club actually paid for my services, he went off and made sure he caught 1000 balls that week. During the weekend game, through the power of repetition, he caught the first five balls that came his way relatively easily and he was back in the game. Through the power of repetition he had replaced his gremlin with his autopilot skill. Repetition is a very important thing and never to be derided or underestimated.

At this point I think it's worth mentioning neuroplasticity. This describes how we create neural-pathways within our brains. Our brains are very complex things but we can exert some control over the thoughts we have and the habits we create. When we have certain thoughts or carry out particular activities over a period of time, we create a neural-pathway around it. The more we think about it or carry out that action or activity, the stronger and more efficient it becomes. Neuroplasticity means that we do actually have the ability to close off old pathways in the brain and create new ones. It seems that you can teach an old dog new tricks and you can do this through removing an old habit and instilling the new one, through focus and repetition. I guess you're programming your autopilot response.

If there is something that creates anxiety in your life, decide what activities you can undertake, apply repetition, face the fear head on, dismantle it and replace it with a much healthier approach that means you won't miss out on new opportunities and experiences. For me, my anxiety was around public speaking. When I first started doing it I was terrified. After three years I started to just about cope. Around 7 years in I started to relax, enjoy it and work on improving my craft. Only now, 14 years on, do I genuinely get self-fulfilment from it, and the fear and anxiety have almost completely subsided. Fourteen years and hundreds of talks and presentations; if I had avoided my fear 14 years ago, I doubt very much if I'd be writing this book today.

The Power of Repetition

1. Nothing fuels greater performance and productivity than 'the power of repetition'.

2. When we practice something again and again we create an 'autopilot' in our brains and can carry out the task or activity with more confidence and less stress.

3. If there is something that creates anxiety in your life, decide what activities you can undertake, apply repetition, face the fear head on, dismantle it and replace with an autopilot.

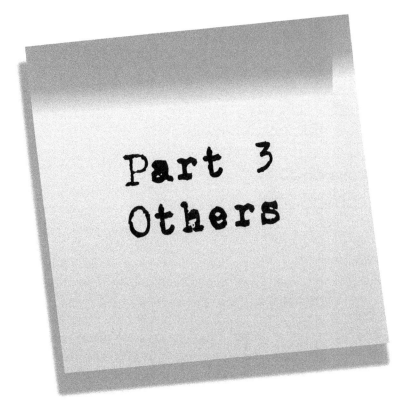

Part 3
Others

Mistake No 23:
Become Socially Excellent

For this important section we're back building on the first chapters of this book around our human iceberg and the importance of emotional intelligence.

Dissecting our human iceberg will help us become more self-aware through the understanding of our sense of purpose and core motivators. From here we can start to see and understand our behaviours more clearly, both productive and counterproductive, and if we can bring emotional intelligence into our conscious then we have all the ingredients to become socially excellent.

I define social excellence as the ability to adapt, thrive and excel in any social environment or interpersonal situation. It also brings in the four influential brain chemicals again: dopamine, oxytocin, serotonin and cortisol, and the ability to manage and influence the release of these chemicals in ourselves and others. So, how do we make some subtle changes that will make a big difference? Let me share with you what I observe in socially excellent people and the 10 top things that they say or do.

1. **Socially excellent people adopt an 'enchant everyone' approach.** When we meet others for the first time, one of three things tends to happen. Firstly, we may take the middle ground and remain neutral as we assess the other person. This means we will be neither overly friendly, nor too cold, just neutral and responsive. If our motivators are predominantly to keep safe and guard against what might go wrong, we will be especially good at taking this neutral position. People have to earn our trust and respect before we will return it. Our brains will be working out if this new person is a likely friend or a foe and if they're worth our time; however, be cautious, in so doing we may also come across as distant and cold and this can actually inhibit our ability to connect to others and establish rapport.

   The second position we may take, and remember we form our opinion of others within the first 10 seconds on how they look, carry themselves and speak etc, could be to repel that person from the outset. If we feel (and we're feeling, not necessarily thinking with the logical part of our brain, in these first moments, right?) that this stranger to us, this new person, may not be trusted, we will repel their advances through our verbal and body language from the start. We may make no effort to talk to them, we'll hang back, we won't engage or we'll quite literally turn our backs on them and talk to someone else. This is also a dangerous approach, as 10 seconds is nowhere near long enough to make an informed opinion about another human being. We've all made decisions about people that we've later acknowledged were off the mark.

   Socially excellent people, on the other hand, adopt the third position in that they simply deploy an 'enchant everyone' approach. They go on the offensive when they meet people. This is not to say that when they have got to know someone better after that initial flurry of assessment, they find that this person is negative and therefore retract accordingly. I'm just talking here about those initial moments of meeting and connection and the opportunity they may hold.

   From my perspective, everybody I meet in life I want to get

to know. When I meet them for the first time it's a golden moment in that I have no idea what they might be able to do for me and what I could do for them. It could be a business opportunity, a new friend, maybe a great tradesman I could call upon. I'm not going to make a hasty decision to steer clear or ignore them: just think what I might be throwing away. This social mastery is something I have worked on and it's what I see in the great communicators. They don't remain neutral, nor repel too quickly until someone has proven themselves. They simply get on the offensive with the single aim of building rapport and enchanting others. This is the first step to becoming socially excellent.

2. **Socially excellent people master the first 10 seconds.** Using non-verbal communication (their body language), socially excellent people are relaxed and open. They don't invade anyone's personal space but give good eye contact with genuine and warm facial expressions, to those they know and especially those they don't. A handshake, particularly in the UK, is an instant way to create a good, warm connection. Not crushing the blood out of someone's fingers, or a weak moist flap, but a warm, assured clasp. This combination of attention, engagement and focus from someone we don't know immediately makes us think 'friend'.

3. **Socially excellent people make the early exchanges entirely about the OTHER person**. They make it personal straightaway, often saying: "Hi, it's great to meet you." Their focus is on you and they want you to know that and, importantly, they don't introduce their own agenda too early. They introduce themselves but put the focus on you immediately, making you feel good and releasing a little bit of serotonin in your brain. This chemical has the effect of making you predisposed to them; you like them immediately. They may go on to ask you, "Where have you travelled from today?" "Tell me a little bit about yourself" to open out the conversation, but it's never about them.

Remember earlier we looked at how important it is when we're with people to be present? Socially excellent people are present, they are actively listening to you, not just waiting for their turn to talk and put their point across. What's going through your mind when you meet a new person? Are you impatient for them to stop talking so that you can get on to (in your mind at least) more important things? If that's the case, you're not listening actively and it will show. Be patient, be present.

4. **Socially excellent people capture, remember and use people's names.** We've all been there; having previously been introduced to someone and when we meet them again, even a few minutes later, maybe a few days, we can't remember their name. It's a frustration many of us share and I know its happened to me! Remembering names, however, is an important thing to do, as it's a powerful way to make others pay attention to you, engage with you and begin to trust you. Good sales people will capture a client's name at the beginning of a meeting and 10 minutes in, when the client has introduced an interesting point, will use it, for example, "You know what, Susan, that's a really interesting point, I agree with what you're saying and here's how we handle that type of request…" Susan's now in no doubt that she is being acknowledged and listened to; she likes that and, in turn, will listen more closely to what the sales person has to say. There is nothing worse than forgetting someone's name after they have addressed you by yours. If you find yourself time and again responding with "Hi there…er, mate" then you need to start paying attention and capture people's names.

5. **Socially excellent people spot and mirror body language**. As well as using names, the mirroring of body language is another highly effective way of creating good rapport. When I began writing this book, I would be in a room with my editor, Jacky, and I would be standing up, delivering my thoughts, pretty much 'presenting' to her, while she sat

at a desk listening and taking notes. I quickly realised that we created the best content when I sat opposite her. It felt far more collaborative and peer-to-peer; it evened out the power-play (if one existed) and we made better progress. I even lowered my volume because I know I'm loud and expressive, while Jacky is soft and analytical. Once we redressed the balance, our work became more conversational.

> *"Yes, I'm a lot quieter than you Martin. You stalking about the room was entertaining but, you're right, we get more done when we both sit and I can think as I listen to you. We found a good pace. I feel it also makes you more reflective and I can get more insight into your ideas."*

There you go, direct input! Mirroring Jacky's position helped create the right pace for our work. It also helped me do a better job for Jacky, as well as creating a good working relationship for us both.

When you are next in a restaurant or at a dinner party, watch your opposite's body language. When they reach for their glass, you reach for yours. Do this for, say, 10 minutes, then switch it up. You pick up your glass and see if they begin to mirror you. If you are in sync, building rapport, they will follow your lead. This mimicking can go unnoticed but, again, it plays a key role in building rapport and trust. You're signalling that you're not a threat, you're on their side and, importantly, you're listening to them.

6. **Socially excellent people remove themselves from negative people or situations.** These masters of communication have the ability to lower and raise their game and extricate themselves from negativity at all costs. Yes, they still adopt an 'enchant everyone' approach, after all they are keen to discover who you and are what you know, BUT, they are also highly attuned to bullshit and low energy black holes. They don't keep negative people in their lives and if they can't remove them completely, they will stay clear of them as much

as possible. The arrogant show-offs are one thing, the black holes can be more stealthy. They are the people who drain your energy, dragging you into their issues, sapping your strength and, worst of all, making you feel negative about yourself. Not always as easy to spot straightaway, but when you come across them it's never too early to move away!

7. **Socially excellent people smile, a lot...** Smiling triggers a mirror reaction from the person you're smiling at. They can't help it. Unless they have some real issues with you, it's instinctive to reciprocate. On meeting others for the first time, if you give them a warm and genuine smile they can't help but smile back. When we are in a rush and arrive somewhere a bit flustered and distracted, a warm open smile is the last thing on our minds, but it should be the first. It helps set the tone. Smiling is endearing, it gets a good reaction and puts people at their ease. It's a great place from which to build a productive relationship.

8. **Socially excellent people have high levels of emotional intelligence.** Perhaps you feel that with all the points before this, this is a given, but emotional intelligence encompasses a great deal more. In pole position is empathy, closely followed by emotional recognition, service and understanding group and power dynamics. These types of people watch and listen first. They gauge the situation and then react accordingly. They spot the extroverts and those who are the influencers in the group. They see the quiet yet determined ones and identify any negative troublemakers early on. In my experience as a speaker and presenter, I quickly learnt to uncover and respond to group and power dynamics within a room so that everyone in my session would get the most from it. We wouldn't be sidetracked by the antics of a few who didn't want to be there or thought they knew better. Switching on the emotional intelligence radar in social situations is crucial if you are going to get the most out of any experience.

9. **Socially excellent people get stuff done.** Now, at this point I can feel many of you all breathing out in a long sigh… Yes, life would be so much easier if those we live and work with just got stuff done (and that's got to include us). Socially excellent people make a point of not letting people down. The big things and the little things - they all matter. When we have a reputation for getting things done, it's an instant trust and confidence builder. When people do what they say they'll do for us, our brains release oxytocin. We are satisfied, content and it builds a great level of rapport. My father's favourite saying is "My word is my bond". There is a lot to be said for that.

10. **Socially excellent people empower others.** Again we have touched on this before and it's worth underlining here. Good communicators and strong leaders make other people feel significant and valued. They elevate others' status and make them feel good about themselves. It's a great quality that really can bring the best out in others and, subsequently, make our lives easier. When we empower others they will often go that extra mile for us, which neatly brings us on to our next chapter: reciprocation.

Become Socially Excellent

1. Social excellence is the ability to adapt, thrive or excel in any interpersonal or social environment.

2. Study the top 10 things that socially excellent people say or do.

3. Start adopting an 'enchant everyone' approach, because right there and then in that moment, you don't know what that person may be able to do for you or you for them.

Mistake No 24:
Understand The Importance of Reciprocation

A short but important chapter! We've looked at many techniques and tools throughout the earlier chapters of this book and reciprocation, the art of the payback or, in other words, 'do something for me I'll do something for you' mindset is another area where I think humans can get it badly wrong.

My research and experience in this area has led me to conclude that there are two types of reciprocation in this world. Conditional and unconditional. Having served in the military and operated in the world of business, I have experienced and observed both first hand.

In the military, reciprocation is entirely unconditional. It doesn't matter if I have served with you for 24 hours and someone else for 24 years, I am prepared to risk my life for you both. It's a difficult thing to explain but it's a value that is instilled in all service personnel throughout training and deployment. In the

We must understand the importance of reciprocation, and we must go first!

military I was paid the least amount of money I have ever earned in my life but I have never experienced camaraderie like it, largely born out of the understanding that the man or woman you are serving with, whether you know them or not, whether you like them or not, would give their life so that you could survive without question, at any time. It's a bond like no other.

The essence of business, however, is completely conditional. I give you a product or service and you give me money. You do something for me, I'll do something for you. As much as I like my clients, if they don't pay me I will struggle to continue doing business with them, therefore, I won't deliver them my services. However, there is a subtle difference we can make that can change our outlook and create more opportunities.

I believe that even given the conditional nature of business reciprocation, we have an incredible opportunity to exploit.

But, we must go first!

We have to start going first in business and in life, and start doing things for other people 'without strings'. Too often I see and hear people saying, "Well, what have they done for me?" as a reason for not supporting or helping someone. Too often we do get dragged into a mindset of conditional reciprocation and wonder why we are waiting for things to happen. The most successful people I observe have this absolutely nailed down.

If I think of all the clients that I work with, the suppliers I engage and the environments I've ever operated in, the people that I see getting on and really achieving things have mastered the art of initial unconditional reciprocation. They are socially excellent people. They reach out to every corner of their business and they build allies by doing something for them first. They go to HR and build an ally, they visit Finance and build an ally; they wander into Production and build allies. And when they need support they've got it – they're the first in the queue to be paid, their emails are responded to faster, they've got the right person's ear.

Along with this ability to foster great relationships and build a 'favour bank' to draw upon, I always remember a great piece of advice by author and professor of psychology and marketing Robert Cialdini[20]. When you do go out and do something for someone first, and the person says, "Thank you", never say, "You're welcome." Instead always respond with, "It's OK, I know you'll do the same for me." You're saying that's OK, I'm genuinely happy to help because I feel you're like me and will give me a hand should I need it one day. You're not saying the person absolutely has to, but you are planting the seed for reciprocation in the future and strengthening the relationship.

Recently a great client of mine went out of his way to recommend my company and my services to one of his customers. Subsequent to this introduction, we negotiated a great new contract and revenue opportunity. My client didn't have to do that and yet he put time and effort into helping me without any expectation of reward.

Two weeks later and I am at a charity auction. Four tickets

were up for grabs to the VIP box at the Millennuim Stadium in Cardiff for the Wales v New Zealand rugby game. Now, I know that my client and his fellow director love their rugby. Even if these tickets cost me £1,000, it's a great way to show my appreciation to my client who was instrumental in my business winning a big new contract.

I made the winning bid and sent the VIP tickets over to my client, simply saying because of what you did for me, please accept these tickets as a show of gratitude. Happily he was amazed and delighted. From his unconditional act, our relationship has been strengthened and elevated into a completely different place. Let's get much smarter about reciprocation. Why is it that you like some of your colleagues and you don't like others? When I ask people this question, they often respond, "Because it's always all about them." Don't make it all about you, be generous where you can, with time, your expertise and resources, and enjoy the rewards it brings. Good will always comes back around in the end.

The Importance of Reciprocation

1. There are two types of reciprocation in this world: conditional and unconditional.

2. We must embrace unconditional and we must go first!

3. Start reaching out to everyone in your life and business and do something for them first. Good will always comes back around in the end.

Mistake No 25:
Coach, Support and Develop Others

You may be wondering why this forms a chapter of the book. I see it as an obligation of being human, a good human, to support, coach and develop others where we can. It's a fundamental strength of ours that we can build and pass on our knowledge and experience. We are nothing in isolation and everything when we collaborate.

> **"No man is an island, entire of itself;**
> **every man is a piece of the continent, a part of the main."**
> John Donne, Devotions 1624

Sometimes we may feel it's not our place, we might say to ourselves, "Who am I to counsel or coach another?" Well, we're all unique, we've all got different experiences and strengths, we've all got something to give. We should never be shy of genuinely wanting to help and support each other, it's how we've survived as long as we have as a species. Even though as social creatures we are programmed to help each other, there are times when we can get trapped in our own self-importance, and it should be noted those who support others tend to achieve self-fulfilment far more quickly than those who do not.

Whether it's with our partners, our children or our colleagues, there are plenty of positive ways in which we can help support and coach others. Through working with some of the UK's best leaders and sports coaches, I have broken it down and created a model that looks at four coaching levels.

1 **The first level is to help someone develop a skill or ability.** We do this with our siblings, children and colleagues. We teach them how to throw a ball, catch a ball, tie their shoelaces, fill in a form, operate a piece of machinery. It's a single skill.

2 **The second level is similar but involves teaching a technique.** Techniques are defined as more about the process and methodology of achieving a desired outcome; approaches and a combination of skills - putting it all together if you like.

I find that 99.9% of coaching in business and in sport is based largely around these first two levels, but there are two more levels that are rarely exploited, but which can really make all the difference.

3 **The third level is around beliefs.** This is the ability to coach people to think differently; to instil a different belief in someone is tricky to do, but can be very powerful if achieved.

4 **The fourth level is changing habits and behaviours.** This is where we look to coach people to formulate positive and habitual patterns of behaviour, which drives long-lasting change and, ultimately, instils or reinforces a set of personal values.

So, levels one and two are quite straightforward: highly practical and actionable. If you have experience, you can teach another a skill and help them improve their technique in its execution. As we know, in time we can improve our skills through repetition. If we neglect them, they get worse. Skills and techniques, lots of people deliver this type of coaching. The real opportunity, however, is helping others with their beliefs and habits because this is where we can help them form long-lasting, productive change. The effects of a new skill or better technique, without repetition, may last a few weeks. On the other hand, productive beliefs and habits can last a lifetime. So how do we then go about coaching at the different levels?

For levels one and two, coaching on skills and techniques, I use the Show, Participate, Observe method, combined with the power of three:

1. **I show someone how to do something and I demonstrate the skill three times.**

2. **We do it together 50/50. You do a bit, I'll do a bit, I am there to 'hold your hand' and we do it this way three times.**

3. **I then stand back and let you do it on your own. When you've done it three times successfully, you're on your way.**

You can then repeat what you've learnt over and over again to perfect the skill. As your coach I'm then going to measure what you're doing to help you improve and keep going forward.

One of my most fulfilling coaching experiences was when I taught my children to swim and ride their bikes. This sits firmly in level one and two. I'll never forget that feeling when they went from my arms and swam for the first time, or I let go of the back of the saddle and they successfully wobbled off, self- powered and didn't immediately fall over. This Show, Participate, Observe method I recommend to anybody who wants to teach a skill. Don't miss a step. Cement all the stages before moving on and it will work well.

In sales training, putting a new sales person in the field with a phone and laptop who doesn't know the products, services and customers very well is as dangerous as it is unkind. You've got to use the Show, Participate and Observe method. Sales Managers have a duty to take them along to meetings, introduce them to customers, show them how to sell the products and services. Then accompany them and take meetings together, finally, simply be there as an observer, as the new sales person conducts the meetings themselves. After the third meeting of flying solo, the new salesperson is truly ready to go into the field, fully confident of their skills and abilities. When we have used this method in business, it has increased productivity of the new recruits tenfold. If you have been in your sector ten years, how can you expect a new sales person to even begin to match what you do with no coaching? You wouldn't chuck your child in the pool and say:

"There you go, you're seven so you should be able to swim by now..." would you?

Show, Participate, Observe. It works really well in pretty much every trade: engineering, manufacturing, sales and certainly when we teach our children. Of course, there are a few things to avoid. There is no point moving on from one element until it has been successfully understood and mastered. Sometimes people are just not ready to be set off, like the child who is not ready to swim by themselves unsupported. In this case you must be prepared to extend the number of repetitions in the Observe section, possibly even the Participate section. It's whatever that individual needs. BUT here's the golden rule – and one that 99% if not 100% of coaches get wrong. When you have gone through the Observe section and the person just isn't getting it, DO NOT go back to Show. It's the worst thing you can do. Can you imagine the scene? "Come on, get out of the way, let me show you

Don't let go if they're not ready – cement all the stages before moving on.

again…" For that person it is going to be humiliating and they will lose whatever confidence they have gained. You may have to go back to Participate but instill in them the confidence to carry on and keep going – that's the art of great coaching for skills and techniques.

As you can imagine, levels three and four require a different approach. Think right back to the beginning of the book and our human iceberg, how our beliefs and behaviours are rooted in our sense of purpose and motivators, sculpted by our experiences. If our job, therefore, is to inspire and trigger behavioural change, it's not about demonstrating, dictating or telling. Level three and four are achieved by engagement and understanding. Without understanding how people think, feel, act and behave, we won't be able to properly engage with them. If we can't engage, we are not going to inspire any change. If we are going to coach anyone on their beliefs, behaviours and habits, whether it's our children, friends, staff or colleagues, we not only have to understand where they're coming from, we must also live and breathe those beliefs and values ourselves.

I see people all the time trying to alter people's mindset and behaviour - making bold statements, giving them reasons why they should do this and that, things they don't hold true to or do themselves. This is a doomed venture on both sides. If we are going to coach at level three and four we must lead by example in everything we do or say. That is the only way people will truly replicate it, when they admire it. Finally, if we want to trigger and inspire productive and long-lasting habits and behaviours, we need to recognise and reward those behaviours when they arise. Recognition and reward releases dopamine in our brains and gives us a great feeling that we want to replicate. We're going to want to try harder and do it again, 'Tough Love' is of limited, short-term use and leaves feelings of negativity behind, even resentment.

Given we agree with this approach, why then in life do we get so caught up reprimanding what's going wrong and not recognising and rewarding the good behaviours we want to encourage? I reckon it's like parenting and I found out, as with many things in my life, the hard way.

Parenting is the hardest thing I've ever done (or ever will do!) My wife and I discuss this all the time. We have three wonderful children and it can be chaos at times. By our own admission, we make mistakes. We get caught in the trap of, "Don't DO that. Stop crying. Stop smacking the TV with the golf club. Stop swinging on your chair…" We are constantly trying to eradicate the 'wrong' behaviour, and our recognition and reward of really good behaviour, which does happen, is, I think, out of balance at times.

Psychology suggests that we have a far better chance of getting our children to adopt good habits and behaviour by ignoring the wrong behaviour (hard when they are having a meltdown in a supermarket) and focusing on the recognition and reward of good habits and behaviour. Children and adults are all human and all respond in a similar way. The fastest way to instil positive habits is to lead by example, recognise and reward. Too often, employers get the balance wrong. They miss opportunities to recognise, elevate and reward someone in front of the team, to say, "Great job Helen" or "Great deal John." When a customer complains, or there is an issue, they are much quicker off the mark to reprimand, worst of all to do it in front of others. And they wonder why they can't embed better behavioural change in their team who are all too beaten up and resentful to engage with them. If we want to coach people to form positive and habitual patterns of behaviour that last a lifetime, we need to live those same values while rewarding and recognising the behaviours in others that we want to foster.

Coach, Support and Develop Others

1. Understand the four coaching levels: skills, techniques, thoughts and habits

2. Use the 'show, participate, observe' method when coaching others.

3. Start focusing on reward – and achievement-based coaching, rather than a consequence and reprimand philosophy, to perform tasks and activities effectively.

Mistake No. 26

Understanding the Six Types of Mindset

This part of the book is relevant to more or less any business sector or industry, and it will probably resonate with people in your personal life as well. Over the years at Trans2 Performance, we have done a great deal of research into people, leadership qualities and all the facets of what we need to improve and foster greater productivity. Through this work we also became fascinated with the different types of mindset that people in businesses displayed - how it's easier to work with some more than with others.

As part of our work with businesses, we carry out a range of cultural surveys and diagnostics. We also get to spend a lot of time in one-to-ones with employees where they are encouraged to tell us anything and everything in confidence without management in the room. We grill them, asking questions like: "What do you like about this company?" "What don't you like?" "Tell me how you feel when this happens in the business?" "How much

Alpha Wolf

Dominant and directive mindset, absolute conviction that their way is the best way. Often operates alone. Resistant to coaching and support.

Snow White

An innocent victim mindset, completely devoid of accountability, everything is against them and not their fault. Can turn very defensive.

Puppet Master

A well balanced mindset. One who would rather share responsibility and uses resources and others to help drive an outcome. A team player.

Needy Child

An insecure mindset, they always need reassurance and want to sanity check and scenario plan everything they do even if they already have the right answer.

Racing Driver

A very confident, driven mindset, individually competent and operates at a very fast pace, very competitive and intent. Open to taking communication and support along the way.

Heart Surgeon

A very focused mindset, will work at a considered pace and will not be deterred from the task at hand. Glory is not their driver, execution and job satisfaction is.

autonomy do you have?" "Do you have empowerment, is it very process-driven here, do you have ownership?" We also talk about how decisions are made and how they feel. Through this we are trying to draw out how they think and what their mindset is within the workplace. We are building an extensive range of data from which we have identified a pattern highlighting six common mindsets of human beings. It is not an exact science, yet we see these patterns repeated throughout the many businesses we work with. The labels we've given the different mindsets are deliberate, as they are universally understood, as you'll discover. As you read on, think about the people you work with, or friends and family members close to you.

The Alpha Wolf

The Alpha Wolf has a dominant and directive mindset, absolute conviction that their way is the best way, they often operate alone and they are resistant to coaching and support. The Alpha Wolf is the type of mindset which says, "I know best, you can't teach me, I've got the experience, I know what I'm doing..." and, quite often, frustratingly, the Alpha Wolf can sometimes be a top performer or a very competent person. In this case their success reinforces their mindset and behaviour. The management teams seem desperate to keep these people because of what they do, but it's difficult as they're such a pain in the arse, they don't stick to the rules, they're outspoken, generally negative and won't take any advice. An Alpha Wolf really is a fascinating beast. They live or die on their performance sword, and have been proven to be uncoachable, displaying a fixed mindset and closed loop thinking. However, they can be great performers and very influential in the workplace.

The Snow White

Snow Whites are completely devoid of accountability, everything's against them and errors or underachievement are definitely not their fault. The company is rubbish, their pay is rubbish, they don't get enough training, have enough equipment or staff. It's everybody and everything's fault barring their own. They will literally use anything to say "I cannot achieve this because of this". Snow Whites can be draining and display a victim mentality mindset in the workplace.

The Puppet Master

Puppet Masters have a well-balanced mindset. Real team players, they are people who would rather share the responsibility, work as a team and use the resources and the people around them to drive an outcome. Think social excellence and its combination of emotional intelligence, enchanting manners and reciprocation, and that's your Puppet Master. They generally have it in abundance. They absolutely understand the importance of working as a team and think, if I can drive an output with little effort, good on me! Far less of a control freak than the Alpha Wolf.

The Needy Child

The Needy Child has an insecure mindset, they lack confidence and always need reassurance, even if they already know what they're doing. It's people in the workplace who come and say, "I'm just letting you know that I've done this, this and this and then next I'm going to do this…" and you respond, "Yes, all right, get on with it, you've been doing it great for the last five years, you know what you're doing, you don't have to check in with me every time...". This mindset is one in which they constantly need reassurance. Often, these people may be responding to core motivators that dictate that they must not make a mistake. Great people who can absolutely perform to a high standard, but they can nonetheless consume the time of the manager and can hinder their own ability to work at a faster pace.

The Racing Driver

Racing Drivers are very confident, driven and independent with a consciously competent mindset, they operate at a very fast pace and can operate happily alone. You may think they are very similar to an Alpha Wolf but there is a fundamental difference. Racing Drivers are open to coaching and support along the way. In fact the Racing Drivers will help you mentor and coach others. The Alpha Wolf, on the other hand, is fixed, closed and not interested in their self-improvement. Nor will make any effort to advance anyone else's.

The Heart Surgeon

Heart Surgeons have a very methodical and focused mindset, they will work at a considered pace and will not be deterred from the task at hand. Glory is not always their driver, execution and job satisfaction is. You can't rush a Heart Surgeon. We gave them this name because if you were having open-heart surgery you would not want an Alpha Wolf or a Racing Driver and you definitely wouldn't want a Snow White. You would want the person who would be methodical and focused on the execution of the job at hand to the highest degree, and they're not going to be rushed. There can be frustration with these mindsets in the workplace, and that usually stems from them being in the wrong role. A Heart Surgeon won't thrive in a high-pressure new business development sales role for example. They will be great, however, as a key account manager looking after customers, doing account plans and strategies. You can imagine the mindset of a Heart Surgeon links to the unconscious motivators to be perfect, correct and right, or to be knowledgeable and smart. These people are analytical: they believe in logic, structure and process, and their main focus is doing things properly.

When we have run through these mindsets with managers, their jaws literally hit the floor and they start writing down lists of their team members in whom they immediately identify these traits. To be a good manager of a team with many different mindsets, it's your job is to be a social chameleon and tailor your approach to them. It's about looking for ways that they can better use their talents, and it is sometimes even about moving them on or out.

Spotting different mindsets is one thing, dealing with them is another; let's have a look at what to do, or perhaps more specifically, how to approach, engage and influence an individual displaying these different types of behaviour.

Dealing with an Alpha Wolf

The worst thing you can do to an Alpha Wolf is challenge them or their opinions, especially in front of a group, as they fundamentally believe they are utterly capable and almost always right. So, a directive or challenging approach will only trigger a completely counterproductive response. I see it in the workplace all the time. Leaders and managers meeting the Alpha Wolf head on in a bid to wrestle back control or drive compliance. This only results in an even more dominant reaction, and the negative effects of this can spread throughout the immediate team or the wider culture of an organisation.

If we are to effectively engage and influence an Alpha Wolf then we must get smart and take a completely different approach, especially if they're a top performer. We must take a more amiable approach; let them have their say and acknowledge their opinions and thoughts, this will instantly reduce the resistance and lower their shield a little. Then it's time to have an almost peer-to-peer discussion, it's time to get visionary. The only way they will tow the line, stick to the rules or come on your journey is if they decide they are going to. So we cannot force change upon them, we can only request it, and the greatest way to do that is to sell them the vision: tell them the stories, talk about outcomes - why we are doing this in the first place, what the end game is and, most importantly, what's in it for them.

When an Alpha Wolf has clear sight of the prize or end game and can link it to their own personal gain, they almost always become, at best less combative and more engaged, at worst more manageable.

Dealing with the Snow White

Snow Whites generally have a victim mentality that may initially be driven by core motivators such as guarding against danger, risk or the fear of failing, but for some reason it has now consumed them. Snow Whites want to rid themselves of any accountability and, quite often, there is only one way to break this pattern. GIVE THEM INSTRUCTION, ACCOUNTABILITY AND A TIME FRAME TO IMPROVE!

Now this may seem harsh, but I have witnessed managers and leaders using every other communication or management style in the book with the Snow White to no avail. When someone has got themself into this closed loop, fixed mindset, defensive state of mind, as with the Alpha Wolf, only they can or will decide to change. But getting visionary or more amiable with the Snow Whites doesn't work. They will find every reason to challenge that vision or take advantage of the amiable nature you display, and life continues as a negative 'moan fest'. This is why it's necessary for them to take some accountability and turn their situation around (or not as the case may be). Snow Whites almost always become their own worst enemy and we find that most people who are exited or dismissed from their roles within businesses do so under a Snow White mindset. Some, however, do have that light bulb moment and drag themselves out of it. Either way, you need to put the accountability on them to shape up or ship out.

Dealing with the Puppet Master

Arguably the easiest mindset to work with as these 'social masters' are already collaborating, supporting, sharing and open. In this case, reciprocation is incredibly important. If a Puppet Master doesn't receive the same treatment back, they can start to retract and withdraw. We also need to ensure that they are in highly social roles. The ability to work in teams and groups is fundamental to their success, and ensuring they avoid isolation is important. A collaborative management or communication style will always work well with a Puppet Master, but the number one thing we must always remember with these master communicators is that they must be kept in the loop. Puppet Masters thrive on being in-the-know, sometimes so they can share this with others, sometimes just to gossip. Either way make sure you keep them in the know and, ultimately, on-side.

Dealing with the Needy Child

The Needy Child can consume your time if you are not careful and it's worth noting that managers and leaders can also fuel this behaviour if they are not communicating with them in the right way. For example, being too amiable or collaborative with a Needy Child can make it worse:you become their 'crutch'.

The best approach to a Needy Child is a little bit of confidence building, mixed with a smattering of tough love. So, being a little directive with them at times does not hurt, but we must still support and coach them to instil confidence. But, here's the important bit, you must put structured time aside for this coaching and support, otherwise they will take advantage of your good nature. Masters of the 'drive by', you'll find them appearing at your desk unannounced to sanity check everything they are doing and dragging you into their agendas time after time. The only way we can build the confidence of a Needy Child is to retract our input slowly and gradually, and, by setting time aside in the diary for dedicated coaching, it means that they will have periods throughout the week where they have to use their initiative.

Dealing with the Racing Driver

The rule of thumb with Racing Drivers is to be clear, be concise, tell them what the goal is and when you want it done by, then kindly move aside! Racing Drivers like the same level of independence as the Alpha Wolf in that they are highly competent and don't need checking on. However, unlike Alphas, they are open to further development and tend to have a real growth mindset, often coming back to you when they need some steer or support. This is the one mindset where we found that adopting a more directive approach is actually appreciated, if not demanded. They want clear instruction and direction so they can press on and make things happen. Racing Drivers are open to being led, advised and communicated with, but can also just get on with the job on their own.

Dealing with the Heart Surgeon

As I discussed earlier, with this particular mindset you must ensure that you have a Heart Surgeon in the right role. Driven by core motivators of perfectionism, standards and accuracy, Heart Surgeons need to be able to take their time with any task. If you have employed a Heart Surgeon into a fast-paced, time-bound or target-driven environment such as sales or manufacturing, they may start to struggle with the quality versus quantity dilemma.

When communicating with a Heart Surgeon you have to deal largely in facts, knowledge and data, providing full details of a particular event, project or initiative. They may have a thousand questions, so be patient and prepared to give a thousand answers if you want them to deliver exactly what you want. Heart Surgeons cannot be put on the spot for quick decisions or immediate answers, they tend to want to gather evidence, process it and then respond as accurately as possible. Pushing them in meetings or on calls for immediate agreements or decisions will only trigger their counterproductive state. Give them notice, give them time where possible, give them data and they'll do a great job.

What mindset would best describe you in your workplace or profession?

Would your colleagues and/or manager agree?

Why not show them the mindsets and find out?

The Six Types of Mindset

1. Get familiar with the six types of mindset you are likely to encounter in the workplace.

2. Typically, the Alpha Wolf and Snow White can present the greatest challenge.

3. Start preparing and adapting your style accordingly to deal with the right mindset in the right situation, with the right response.

Mistake No 27:
Deploy The Three Circle Theory

When you work with many different people during one-to-one development sessions, they open up to you about what really motivates them, affects them and triggers counterproductive behaviour and, importantly for this chapter of the book, who has this influence over their lives.

In most cases people talk about those close to them; partners, family members and life-long friends. Because of these strong connections, the impact of their actions is always amplified when it is negative. My observations gave me pause for thought about the influence of family and friends and how we all appear, to a lesser or greater extent, to suffer from draining influences and negativity. So much so that it affects our ability to be content, happy and productive people. I then started to work on my Three Circle Theory to help myself and others find a way to make sense of what was happening and combat the counterproductive influences of those around us.

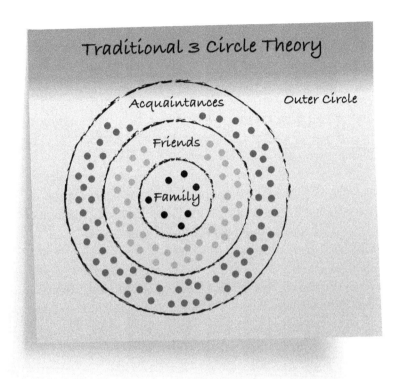

Traditional 3 Circle Theory

We humans seem to be programmed to automatically create in our minds a traditional form of the Three Circle Theory. We tend to place our family within the inner circle. Family first, right!? They are connected to us by blood. Love 'em or hate 'em, you can't pick your family!

Moving outwards, we most often keep our good friends in our close circle. These may be the people we have grown up with, whom we socialise with; best mates, good friends. We choose them for many different reasons, sometimes they seem to choose us and they play a significant role in our lives.

In the third extended circle we place our acquaintances. We know them but not as well. They may be colleagues, customers, somebody you see networking, at yoga or in the pub. Beyond this, in the outer circle, sits everyone else who touches our lives.

Now, here's where I strongly believe we can make a huge difference to our lives in an instant. As I said previously, from my many hours sitting and talking to people from all walks of life I find that, at times, our family members, those we keep closer than anyone else, can sometimes be the most negative people in our lives. They can be the ones who harm us more than support us and, as long as we keep them in that inner circle, they will always have a greater, and at times more detrimental, impact upon us than anyone else.

If you want to begin to change the course of your life, it's time for you to wrestle some control back and for you to choose the people in those circles. Not by blood, tradition, proximity or expectation, but by those who positively impact your life. Those whom you trust 100% and who trust you; those who encourage and support you; who will stand by you even when you're wrong; who will make you feel significant and valued and with whom you would share anything with. This is your true inner circle.

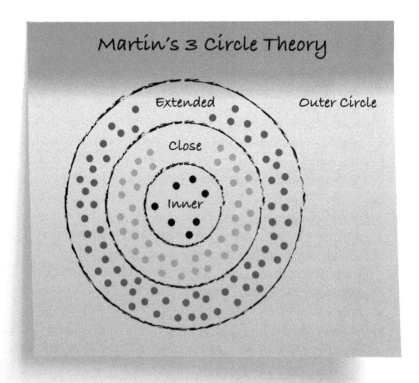

I have just nine people in my **inner circle**. Only six of them are part of my family, and I have a big family! Those nine people positively influence my life more than anyone else. I trust them and they trust me 100%. They encourage me and I know they'll stand by me even when I get it wrong. They value me and I value them. I trust their advice and they listen to me. When you redefine this inner circle for yourself, you have to be completely honest. Get rid of the notion that you 'have' to keep someone in your inner circle because of tradition. This can be difficult if you are an amiable person who likes to please, or someone with a strong belief in family first. The criteria is simply that they must unconditionally and relentlessly be there for you. If they're not there for YOU then they're not in.

Your **close circle** is still a place for the people who are a big part of your life. They hold a particular significance to you and you for them. Their influence on you can be positive and at times it may be negative: you would share most things about yourself with them, but not absolutely everything. There could well be a lot of family members in this circle, which is fine. It doesn't mean just because they are not in your inner circle that you don't love them. Love has nothing to do with this exercise. You can still love people in your close and extended circle. However, they are people who can sometimes have a negative impact on your life. They may judge you and not offer much support; perhaps they say and do things that are not always in your best interest, hence they are close but that's as far as they get.

The third **extended circle** will hold the largest number of people, as this is the place for the people you know reasonably well and who you spend time with periodically for a range of different reasons. You may enjoy being with them or you may dread it. Either way it is usually for short periods of time such as at work, at the sports club, an old school friend, a friend of a friend you see on a night out. They touch your life but not with great impact.

Finally, the outer circle is anyone you have brushed past, nodded to, smiled at or exchanged a few words with on the planet.

Start today with a blank sheet of paper and define your three circles. Think about your family, friends, colleagues, old school pals – everyone you have been associated with. Be honest. People can move between groups throughout your life as your circumstances change. Remember, the acid test for that inner circle is who would encourage and stand by you even when you are wrong?

What's the point of this exercise? It allows you to begin to condition yourself to be only truly affected by the thoughts, words and actions of your true inner circle. This is not to say that you don't listen to anyone in your close or even extended circles. It's important to look at things from another person's point of view, be tolerant of their beliefs and ideas, BUT – and it's a big B U T – if anyone from my inner circle wants to critique what I do or how I do it, I know that they have my best interests at heart. That's the difference between the inner and close circles, and it's a life-defining one.

When you can condition yourself only to be affected, moti-vated or have your actions examined by your inner circle, you will never go too far wrong. These are the only people, whether they are a partner, a brother, sister, best friends, a colleague you met two years ago or a neighbour whom you allow to have a deep emotional impact upon you. Remember it's completely up to you who is in that inner circle and only for you to decide and know.

If you have the wrong people in your inner circle, even though you may love them, they may not always have your best interests at heart. They likely to have a different agenda and one that is more usually about themselves and their lives, and their circle. Too many of us worry about what everyone else is thinking or saying about us, it saps our energy, it reduces our confidence, it makes us procrastinate for days, so here's a way to stop the rot.

I go to my inner circle 'nine' for a warts-and-all discussion about my ideas and my feelings. If I'm off the mark they'll tell me, but they'll also back me up whatever I decide. I value their opinion and they know it and I do the same for them, no ques-tions asked. I choose my close circle from the significant and im-portant people in my life, those I love, whom I talk with, discuss and debate, but I don't get hung up on their deep thoughts, feelings and intentions, because they are in my close circle for a reason. I'll listen to them, I'll support them if they need it, but if someone in that close circle wrote me off or was negative about me, I won't lose any sleep over it. It could be coming from a place of judgement, jealousy or low-level negativity because it might inconvenience them or not align with their views. **I've made a decision around those to whom I am truly listening and those whom I'm only willing to hear**. Like the old boss who wrote me off when I wanted to start my business, he wasn't in my inner nine and therefore he didn't deter me. In fact, he encouraged me.

The extended circle could be open to everyone you meet throughout your life. There may even be someone in there who in a few years' time will be right with you in your inner circle, who knows?

This is a great exercise to do and it can change your life and the way you view others. Because I GUARANTEE that you have people in your inner circle right now who, to some extent, are a toxic or negative influence on your life. I also guarantee that it is causing you some severe stress and inhibiting your ability to be happy. It's simple: move them out to the close or extended circle and only be truly encouraged or deterred by those in your inner circle.

Finally, another great benefit of using this model is that it reminds me who I want to spend most of my time with. Life is short and I want to spend it with my close circle but I will always prioritise my inner nine whenever I can and so should you. If you want to move forward and be happy, surround yourself with people who make you the best version of yourself. They won't always tell you you're right and they might pull you up, but they will always have your best interests at heart and will support you no matter what.

Now, to complete the 30 most common mistakes we humans make, I've got three final quick wins to help you succeed in life and business.

The Three Circle Theory

1. We don't have to follow tradition and operate on a family, friends, acquaintances basis.

2. Follow my Three Circle Theory and reorganise your priorities based on the people who have the single greatest impact on your life.

3. Love has nothing to do with this exercise. It's purely about who impacts positively on your life, who supports you; those you just hear, and those to whom you should truly be listening to.

Mistake No 28:
There is Always Danger in Assumption

We make assumptions all the time, every day, possibly every minute. Remember open versus closed loop thinking? An assumption can easily lead us into closed loop thinking because we are pre-determining the results of a scenario as we see it: we assume the outcome.

When we meet someone for the first time there are two things to remember. Just pause for thought and consider…

1. Our limbic system reacts with an immediate gut response to the look and behaviour of that person. We are responding to those feelings and emotions, NOT logic and fact.

2. We don't know this person's human iceberg, their core motivators or sense of purpose. Let's face it we are just scratching the surface of our own regardless of anyone else's!

Here are just a few classic examples of where we humans let our assumptions get us into a world of trouble. Pause for thought after reading them and decide if this presents an opportunity for you to make a change.

1. Assuming something is personal

When we encounter a negative comment or action from someone, we instantly assume that this behaviour is personal. It's a survival instinct. And, because we have assumed that it's personal, we then tend to dwell, procrastinate and over-analyse the hell out of it. This leads to a damaging pattern of behaviour I call 'negative retention.'

The longer our thoughts fester on our assumption that someone has personally wronged us, the more resentment and animosity we build. The more resentment and animosity we build, the more we flood our brains with cortisol, causing further anxiety and stress. Here's a great analogy that explains the effects of negative retention:

The glass in the air

Imagine I am holding a small glass of water up in the air. I then ask you, "How much does this glass of water weigh?" I do this quite a lot in training and consulting sessions with clients. The delegates usually start to respond:

"Five ounces?"

"100 grams?"

The guesses come thick and fast. After five minutes of debate I elaborate, telling them that it doesn't really matter how much the glass actually weighs at all, it only matters how long I hold onto it. Now that I have everyone puzzled, I make the point that if I hold on to the glass for a few moments it will cause me no trouble. If I hold onto it for a few minutes it will start to cause me some mild distress and pain. But if I hold onto the glass for a few hours, it will cause me serious fatigue both physically and mentally. So it really doesn't matter how much the glass weighs. What matters is how long I hold onto it.

The glass in the air simply represents our thoughts and assumptions. If we hold onto resentment or negativity for few moments it will not harm us. If we hold onto it for a few days it starts to inhibit our ability to be happy and productive. If we hold onto it for weeks or months it will literally destroy our wellbeing. Almost always, we tend to assume that stuff happening around us is personal. Well, most of the time it isn't, as we have explored previously in this book. Now, if you are the kind of person who assumes you are being personally attacked time and time again and who holds onto the your natural resentment and anxiety in the form of 'negative retention', this is likely to be having a big impact on your life. And let me tell you, YOU are the only person this impacts, not the people you are thinking about! So do yourself a favour and remember… On most occasions it isn't personal. On most occasions you're assuming the worst as a survival instinct, but on EVERY occasion YOU have the ability to put the glass down.

Go ahead… PUT THE GLASS DOWN.

2. Assuming you will be good or bad at something

There is a great quote by Henry Ford, "If you think you can, or you think you can't - you're right." It's so true. We looked earlier in the book at the Law of Attraction and how thinking positively about an outcome can significantly increase your chances of achieving it. Likewise, thinking negatively can significantly increase your chances of failure. And, if you think about it, this stems from assumption again. We all have that initial feeling of can or can't, will or won't, like or dislike. In our personal lives we do this all the time. When our kids inquisitively ask us what we are eating and we reply, "Oh, it's salmon, but I don't think you'll like it.", we make an instant assumption, possibly based on our own childhood tastes. Not only that, but we have also just planted a seed in our child's mind that they won't like it, even before they have tried!

The same applies when we assume that we would never make

a good sales person, or that we could never write a book, and, my personal favourite, "I don't think I'm built for running!" Let me tell you that all human beings are built for running. We evolved from apes to walk on two legs so that we could watch the horizon for threats, whilst being able to walk and run efficiently with our hands free to carry tools and hunting weapons. Our early ancestors' only mode of speedy transportation was running! Today, the things that make it hard for able-bodied people without illness to run is a little too much weight or we are just unfit! Even then it gets easier with repetition and a good diet. But, if you tell yourself you're not built for running, you're going to be right. If you tell yourself, it will be tough but I can do this and I will become better at it in time, you'll be right.

We have to make sure that we don't just assume something and then let it control our actions and behaviours. This closed loop thinking can all too quickly become a habit and our default response to new or different things is negative and pessimistic. In all probability we'll be missing the opportunity to grow, improve and be happy.

'If you think you can, or you think you can't - you're right'
Henry Ford

There is Always Danger in Assumption

1. Remember our limbic system is trying to give us a fight or flight response in seconds. Be cautious.

2. Never assume something is personal - almost always it isn't, so put the glass down.

3. We should never assume that we will be good or bad at something. If you think we can or you think we can't, you'll be right.

Mistake No 29:
The Lazy Communication Trap

We've looked at how we can communicate better and influence others by being present and actively listening, becoming more emotionally intelligent and mastering the art of social excellence. Yet with the current pace of technology, constant access to social media and super fast connectivity, we can and do get very lazy with our communication. It's hard not to, it's at our finger tips 24/7.

Today, we can pretty much communicate with anyone anywhere and it can be great for business. We can collaborate more easily, purchase faster - same day, never mind next day delivery, so how do we prepare for a world where the millennials growing up with this culture and access will rule? After a day in the office in a very fast-paced environment, dealing with multiple streams of communication that all require our attention, we can get home and feel burnt out. I have done it myself. I land on my sofa and my head feels cloudy, I squint, my forehead feels compressed through concentration and what feels like a herd of buffalo is stampeding through my mind. For many people even struggle to sleep.

For me there are three things I try to do to ensure I don't fall into this trap. I absolutely embrace technology but don't let it rule me and ensure, more so now than ever, that I get the balance of work and home life right.

Firstly, after reading an article on mindfulness, one thing really struck a chord. The need to spend some time every day, even just ten minutes, away from the glowing screens and the relentless calls of a desk-based culture. For me this is my walk to the sandwich shop. Every day, rain or shine, I leave my phone on my desk and walk. I get some air, I focus on my breathing, I drop my shoulders, I relax. My office is close to the Humber estuary in East Yorkshire and the view across the water is a great way to unwind. It's not rocket science but it's worth reminding ourselves that we do our best work when we can recharge our batteries, even for a short while every day. We must remind ourselves to step outside our bubble and find out how the rest of the world is getting on.

Now, I needn't take this walk. I can bring a packed lunch into work, which would certainly be cheaper, but the other reason I won't is because I know I will eat at my desk, checking out my social media. I would be stuck in the communication trap, not resting my brain and not realising that I'm storing up trouble for later.

Secondly, I try to abide by the 6pm Rule, for which I give full credit to my wife. No technology after 6pm. Probably like you I spend my life on screens and technology. Our businesses depend on it; my communication with my teams, my friends, my family, everything relies on technology and with three children at home, who haven't seen me all day, my addiction to it was getting in the way of being present with my family.

One instance sticks in my mind. Having just arrived home after a busy day, my little girl began tugging me on the arm and saying, "Daddy, daddy, daddy..." She'd done something at school that day that she was really proud of and was desperate to show me. As usual I had my head buried in my phone. I said, "One second" which of course it wasn't by the time I had finished my email and went back to her. But the moment had passed, she was not as enthusiastic about what she wanted to tell me, and it broke my heart. The moment of joy was gone for us both.

So, to help get me out of the Lazy Communication Trap, I try to leave my phone on the side at 6pm and not engage in work-related activity again until 6am. I also try to limit my time on social media in that time frame. I try my best and, mostly... mostly I'm succeeding. It changes the whole dynamic and enjoyment of my family time, mainly because I am there with them in body as well as mind.

It's a troubling thought that our children are watching us and picking up our good and our bad habits, especially when it comes to technology.

Thirdly, when I work with any business or individual, I set out a communication policy. If you don't, in my experience, the gloves are off, everyone is on social media, emails are fired in every direction for the slightest of pretexts, everyone is dragging everyone else into their email chains, into their stuff... It's lazy and, ultimately, hugely time-consuming. A communication policy doesn't have to be rigid. In fact mine is very simple and it goes like this:

Email, text, social media or video are for the passing of data, knowledge and information only.

Any conflict resolution, decisions or issues are to be carried out in person.

That's it.

With these two parameters, people have the freedom to do as they please but, if there is a conflict or a disagreement that needs resolving or a key decision that people are struggling to make, an issue that's arisen from a customer or the business, we meet in a room, or worst case we have a telephone conversation, human to human. The outcome is always better. Think about your workplace, your team and your department. Do you have you got any form of Communication Policy? Or is it the Wild West? Is someone two desks away sending you queries by email? Millennials coming into the work place will potentially operate all day, every day, at their PC on email, without speaking to a single human being. You cannot tell me we can build cultures and relationships that drive great productivity and performance operating like that?

Let's embrace technology but remember to keep it as human as possible.

The Lazy Communication Trap

1. Challenge yourself not to get drawn into the lazy communication trap.

2. Adopt the 6pm Rule. No technology after 6pm. It's difficult, but it could change your life. Being present with our families is crucial.

3. Consider a communication policy in the workplace. This could be essential for the future of good and productive human interaction within businesses.

Mistake No 30:
People Don't Always Remember What You Say

When all is said and done, very, very few people will remember everything you say to them. As you reach the end of this book, there will be (I hope) some memorable sections that resonated with you; that you connected with emotionally, that possibly inspired you or made you reflect. It is an important principle in life that the art of building rewarding and mutually beneficial relationships lies in our ability to touch people's hearts and make them feel great - to connect on an emotional level.

For me, writing this book was my way of trying to make a difference. It allows me to be useful, to help others, to pass on what I have learnt through trial and error, through research and collaboration over the last 14 years. Initially, if I'm honest, I first thought of it as an idiot's guide to life for my children. Here you are, the 30 biggest mistakes or opportunities, kids – have a head start! But, since starting my business and having the privilege of working with thousands of people in all walks of life, it's become a much deeper need to share ideas and knowledge with as many people as I can. And here, in a nutshell, is the last nugget I want to share with you.

"At the end of the day people won't remember what you said or did, but they will always remember how you made them feel."
Maya Angelou

Connecting with people on an emotional level, here's how...

1. **Say it and mean it.** Whatever you say to other people, if you are trying to inspire change, it can't just be out of a textbook, it can't be regurgitated, it can't be because it sounds good, you have to sincerely mean it. One little phrase that can make someone's day and is simple to begin with is this: "You know what's great about you...?" Don't be embarrassed to compliment others, tell them, be sincere and mean it.

2. **Tell great stories.** Storytelling is a wonderful, timeless art that captures our attention, illustrates our meaning and engages people in life and in business. Stories release oxytocin and dopamine in our brains, they give us satisfaction, interest and escapism. My friends and I love storytelling. We often sit around reciting stories of our school years or rugby days and spend the entire time laughing. It's an incredibly powerful thing to do, and stories are far easier to remember than facts and figures because they tap into our emotions and keep us engaged.

3. **Let people know that they are not alone.** Throughout all the stresses and strains of our daily lives, we're all just human. We all make mistakes, I've

introduced you to 30 of mine and I'm sure there are more to come. We all share the same challenges and we're all in it together. Stress and anxiety are also more common than you think. Stress is a human instinct, it's a way of alerting us to things that are either a threat or important. Feeling stress or anxiety is not a weakness. Every human on the planet suffers from stress, it's a fact, and if you take time to understand it, it's not all bad and it can be managed and controlled.

Being better at being human…

Sharing knowledge and ideas is an important way to help each other and try to get better at being human. The world is not going to become any less complicated, so, by keeping it human, acknowledging our mistakes and learning from them, I hope this book will help you avoid some of the potholes and bring you the success you're looking for. The lessons I have learned and continue to learn have certainly help me.

If you want to live a happier, more content and self-fulfilled life, then take more time to get to know and develop yourself. Go on a mission to uncover your own human iceberg. Use the 30 mistakes and opportunities from this book as a blueprint, a strategy, and start the process. Understand your brain, appreciate how wonderful it is and the chemicals it releases which influence your actions. Spend your time wisely. Adopt an 'enchant everyone' approach. Actively listen and master the art of reciprocation. Remove the negative people from your life and spend more time with those who have your best interests at heart… And if there is only one thing you take from this book, then please, let it be this:

We are all humans relying on other humans to survive and thrive. The key is to focus on thriving, not just surviving.

People Don't Remember What You Say

1. People won't remember what we say or do, but they will always remember how we made them feel.

2. Say it and mean it - speak from the heart, it engages and inspires others.

3. Become a storyteller - stories capture peoples' imaginations and emotions, allowing you to connect with them on a deeper level.

The Last Word…

Written in the 1930s, this poem by Dale Wimbrow was a feature of my time in the military. Written solely from a man's point of view, it may feel a little dated, yet, for me, it offers a universal truth for every human being whatever our age, gender or job, in our search for a happy, productive and successful life.

The Man in the Glass

When you get what you want in your struggle for self
And the world makes you king for a day
Just go to the mirror and look at yourself
And see what that man has to say.

For it isn't your Father or Mother or wife
Whose judgement upon you must pass.
The fellow whose verdict counts most in your life
Is the one staring back from the glass.

Some people may call you a straight shooting chum
And call you a wonderful guy,
But the man in the glass says you're only a bum
If you can't look him straight in the eye.

He's the fellow to please, never mind all the rest
For he's with you clear to the end,
And you know you have passed your most dangerous test
If the man in the glass is your friend.

You may face the whole world down the pathway of life
And get pats on the back when you pass,
But your final reward will be heartache and strife
If you've cheated the man in the glass.

Acknowledgements

Firstly, I would like to thank my editor Jacky Fitt and book designer Ned Hoste at the Big Ideas Library for your support, encouragement and knowledge. Without you this book would not have been possible.

Thank you to my wife Lucy for your love, support and immovable belief in everything I do and for being a fantastic mother to our children, but mostly for being my best friend, my soul mate and the absolute centre of my inner circle. Thank you to the rest of my inner circle and all my fantastic friends and family whom I love and care about dearly. Especially to my children, Isabel, Nyla and Zander, you inspire and motivate me every day.

I'd also like to thank some other significant people for their influence on my life and career. Thank you Wayne OKell MBE. You took me under your wing at a critical time in my life and were the first person in the military to truly believe in me. I will never forget the words you shared with me, the way you inspired me to channel what I had, putting it to good use. I'd like to also mention Victoria Farmer and Simon Marus for giving me my big opportunity at Gartner; to take a punt on a 25-year-old lad from Hull was risky and this really was the start of my professional success. Thank you for believing in me.

And finally, thank you to all my staff, clients, partners and business associates. Without you I would not be able to do the work I do and make the difference I desire.

Martin Johnson

CEO, Trans2 Performance

Following five years of military service, Martin has occupied senior sales and leadership roles in both small dynamic and large global organisations, including seven years with consulting giant, Gartner. He is now the Co-Founder and CEO of Trans2 Performance and is best known for his talks on organisational culture, leadership and human performance. Martin is also the creator of T2 Talks, a motivational talks event born out of his vision and passion for developing others.

Over the past few years Martin has become a strategic advisor and leading performance coach with large corporations, the military and in the world of professional sport.

Endnotes

[1] Professor Stephen Hawking, CH, CBE, FRS, FRSA: theoretical physicist, cosmologist and author.
http://www.hawking.org.uk page 9

[2] Dr Sigmund Freud: neurologist, author and the founder of psychoanalysis.
https://en.wikipedia.org/wiki/Sigmund_Freud page 13

[3] Dr Edward Deming: American engineer, statistician, professor, author and management consultant.
https://en.wikipedia.org/wiki/W._Edwards_Deming page25

[4] Dr Paul Hertz: statistician, management consultant, architect of PRINT© programme.
http://www.paulhertzgroup.com/about-paul-hertz/ page 25

[5] Professor Steve Peters: psychiatrist and author of *The Chimp Paradox* http://chimpmanagement.com page 32

6   Top Global Fears survey and data sources: page 43
https://www.researchgate.net/publication/271993200_Is_
Public_Speaking_Really_More_Feared_Than_Death

http://www.goodtoknow.co.uk/wellbeing/544550/britain-
top-10-worst-fears

https://www.washingtonpost.com/news/wonk/
wp/2014/10/30/clowns-are-twice-as-scary-to-democrats-as-
they-are-to-republicans/?utm_term=.718d9988036a

7   Jim Rohn: entrepreneur and author page 47
https://en.wikipedia.org/wiki/Jim_Rohn

8   Matthew Syed: journalist, broadcaster and author of *Black
Box Thinking – the surprising truth about success*
http://www.matthewsyed.co.uk/books/ page 50

9   Professor Yuval Noah Harari: historian and author of *Sapiens
A Brief History of Humankind*
http://www.ynharari.com/book/sapiens/ Page 54

10 Dr Daniel Goldman: psychologist, science journalist, lecturer
and author of *Emotional Intelligence and Social Intelligence:
The New Science of Human Relationships.*
http://www.danielgoleman.info page 59

11 Stephen Covey: educator, businessman and author of
The 7 Habits of Highly Effective People.
https://www.stephencovey.com page 63

12 Article/Survey: *Majority of Graduates discount value of soft
skills* by Hayley Kirton, People Management. May 2016
http://www2.cipd.co.uk/pm/peoplemanagement/b/weblog/
archive/2015/05/21/majority-of-graduates-discount-value-
of-soft-skills-finds-survey.aspx#   page 64

[13] *The Power of Vulnerability* TED Talk by Brené Brown: research professor, author and public speaker.
https://www.ted.com/talks/brene_brown_on_vulnerability page 75

[14] Stephen Covey Matrix from *The 7 Habits of Highly Effective People.* https://www.stephencovey.com page 91

[15] *Your Body Language May Shape Who You Are* TED Talk by Amy Cuddy: social psychologist, author and lecturer.
https://www.ted.com/talks/amy_cuddy_your_body_language_shapes_who_you_are page 108

[16] HMS Nottingham
https://en.wikipedia.org/wiki/HMS_Nottingham_(D91)
page 109

[17] Rhonda Byrne: television writer, producer and author of *The Secret.*
http://www.thesecret.tv page 128

[18] Tony Robbins, author, entrepreneur and life coach.
https://en.wikipedia.org/wiki/Tony_Robbins page 136

[19] Professor Steve Peters: psychiatrist and author of *The Chimp Paradox*
http://chimpmanagement.com   page 141

[20] Professor Robert Cialdi: psychologist, speaker and author
https://en.wikipedia.org/wiki/Robert_Cialdini   page 151

Further Reading

The Chimp Paradox by Dr Steve Peters
Published by Vermillion
ISBN-10: 009193558X
ISBN-13: 978-0091935580

The 7 Habits of Highly Effective People by Stephen Covey
Published by Simon and Schuster
ISBN-10: 0684858398
ISBN-13: 978-0684858395

Black Box Thinking by Matthew Syed
Published by John Murray
ISBN-10: 1473613809
ISBN-13: 978-1473613805

Sapiens – A Brief History of Humankind by Yuval Noha Harari
Published by Vintage
ISBN-10: 0099590085

Emotional Intelligence by Daniel Goldman
Published by Bentam Doubleday Dell Publishing Group
ISBN-10: 055384007X
ISBN-13: 978-0553840070

Enchantment by Guy Kawasaki
Published by Portfolio Penguin
ISBN-10: 0241953650
ISBN-13: 978-0241953655

The Inside Out Revolution by Michael Neil
Published by Hay House UK
ISBN-10: 1781800790
ISBN-13: 978-1781800799

Outliers by Malcolm Gladwell
Published by Penguin
ISBN-10: 0141036257
ISBN-13: 978-0141036250

Talk like TED by Carmine Gallo
Published by Pan
ISBN-10: 1509867392
ISBN-13: 978-1509867394